David Hare's first full-length p
Since then he has written over thirty stage plays and thirty
screenplays for film and television. The plays include *Plenty*,
Pravda (with Howard Brenton), *The Secret Rapture*, *Racing
Demon*, *Skylight*, *Amy's View*, *The Blue Room*, *Via Dolorosa*,
Stuff Happens, *The Absence of War*, *The Judas Kiss*, *The Red Barn*,
The Moderate Soprano, *Beat the Devil* and *Straight Line Crazy*.
For cinema, he has written *The Hours*, *The Reader*, *Damage*,
Denial, *Wetherby* and *The White Crow*, among others, while his
television films include *Licking Hitler*, the *Worricker Trilogy*,
Collateral and *Roadkill*. In a millennial poll of the greatest plays
of the twentieth century, five of the top hundred were his.

DAVID HARE

WE TRAVELLED

Essays and Poems

faber

First published in the UK in 2021
by Faber & Faber Limited
74–77 Great Russell Street
London WC1B 3DA

This paperback edition first published in 2022

Typeset by Agnesi Text, Hadleigh, Suffolk
Printed and bound in the UK by CPI Group (UK) Ltd, Croydon CRO 4YY

Some of these essays have been published or excerpted by the *Guardian*, the website
Tortoise, the National Portrait Gallery, the Imperial War Museum, American *Vogue*,
Vintage, the *New Statesman* and Faber & Faber. 'Influence' was first printed
in *Index on Censorship*. 'The Death of Everybody' was first published in the *Financial
Times*. We acknowledge and thank these publications.
All material is copyrighted.

Excerpt from the poem 'A Summer Night' by W. H. Auden from *Collected Poems*,
ed. Edward Mendelson, Faber & Faber, 1976, Copyright © [1933] by W. H. Auden,
renewed. Reproduced by permission of Curtis Brown, Ltd

A CIP record for this book
is available from the British Library

ISBN 978-0-571-36953-9

2 4 6 8 10 9 7 5 3 1

For Nicole
With all my love

From gardens where we feel secure
Look up and with a sigh endure
   The tyrannies of love:

And, gentle, do not care to know,
Where Poland draws her eastern bow,
   What violence is done,
Nor ask what doubtful act allows
Our freedom in this English house,
   Our picnics in the sun.

W. H. AUDEN

CONTENTS

Poems

INTRODUCTION

I can't remember if I had any plans for the twenty-first century. I was already fifty-two when it arrived. But events raced off in such unexpected directions that any possible ideas must have gone out the window. Many of us shared the sensation that history was speeding up. In the theatre, at least, I managed to keep abreast. I wrote plays about three of the significant events. *Stuff Happens* was about the diplomatic process leading up to the invasion of Iraq in 2003. *The Power of Yes* explained the global crisis brought about by the recklessness of bankers in 2008. And when I fell ill early in the pandemic in 2020, I was ideally placed to write *Beat the Devil*, an account of what it was like to experience Covid-19. When presented at the Bridge Theatre, it was, appropriately, the first play to open indoors in London after the first lockdown.

In the same period, film preoccupied me more and more, both for the cinema and for television. Whether the subject was Rudolf Nureyev or Holocaust denial, whether it was Virginia Woolf or the post-war German experience, I was happy to stick with being screenwriter only. Over a three-year period, I worked on twenty-one drafts of Jonathan Franzen's novel *The Corrections*, without the film getting made. But in 2011, I realised I wanted to direct again. My outrage at British complicity in torture and rendition inspired me to write and direct three spy films, *Page Eight*, *Turks & Caicos* and *Salting the Battlefield*. Next, my relationship with the BBC led me, for the first time, into writing a television series. It was interesting to tackle a new skill so late in life. *Collateral* was fired by outrage at the inhumane British system of detaining asylum seekers while they waited for appeal – a system which has only got worse in the past year. *Roadkill* followed, like *Collateral*, in four one-hour parts. The Conservative Party had recently formed their sixth successive government in a row. I was bewildered why nobody else wrote much about them, and why their values went unexamined.

Because I took time out in the middle of all this to write a memoir, *The Blue Touch Paper*, I was able to compare the rewards of working alone with the rewards of working in company. Novelists or biographers always seemed to be missing half the fun of writing. Surely you want to enjoy your ideas being enriched by others. But I admit that I had begun, after forty years, to find the constant demands of collaborative forms exhausting. A couple of bad experiences with disappointing colleagues made me scratchy. The silence of the study became attractive after a whole lifetime in the hurly-burly of the rehearsal room and the script meeting. My collaborative gene was beginning to get frayed. But after the young stage director Robert Icke had lent his authority to my version of a Simenon novel, *The Red Barn*, and after the young film director SJ Clarkson had performed equal magic on *Collateral*, I realised that working with a new generation had refreshed me. By the time the even younger Kate Hewitt – born long after the play was written – had put a glow on my 1978 play *Plenty* in an accomplished production in Chichester, my delight in teamwork was fully restored.

Needless to say, it was the performances of the actors in all these various works which sustained me through darker moods.

However, there was a lot I wanted to describe which no longer belonged in public forms. That's the reason I started writing poetry. It had two advantages. First, the knowledge that I was writing without the intention of ever being published gave me freedom. There's nothing more liberating than knowing your baby steps will never see the light of day. But second, I was able to answer my wife, Nicole Farhi, when she jokingly complained that I never wrote about her.

It is true that my work has rarely been autobiographical. My emotional experiences inform the way I think about any subject – how can they not? – but I can't say I've ever felt much need, except in my school play *South Downs*, to portray my own life and relationships. It's not my thing. But I did find that I was nursing a strong urge to put this extraordinary woman to whom I was married on the page. I also wanted to express the love I felt for her. Such impulses may well be naive, but there we are. We're given our subject, we don't choose it, and my love for Nicole was mine.

I knew that in writing poetry I was climbing in through the off-street window of a club of which I am not a member. At Cambridge University in the 1960s, I'd studied in the School of English when it was at its most grudging and cheerless. I knew at first hand how prescriptive the world of poetry could be. I had learned there that there was no expression, however articulate, to which yet more articulate objection could not be made – and was. Like the friend I mention in the essay 'A Twenty-First-Century Lexicon', I was occasionally congratulated on my courage in daring to write the stuff at all. How could anyone who wasn't in touch with the state of the art even begin to contribute to it? How could I walk into such a thorny place without wearing a protective suiting of scholarship?

For some years I thought publication might spoil the pleasure of writing poetry. But my mind was changed by coming across Auden's definition. He called poetry 'memorable speech'. This description excited me, because it manages to be both generous and incredibly demanding at the same time. I chose first to publish some poems in a private edition which I distributed to friends in 2017. But since then, I've continued to write, almost always on impulse and as the mood took me. A curtain call at a Broadway play with Philip Seymour Hoffman might send me off to my notebook as unexpectedly as the dangerous roundabout at the north end of Lambeth Bridge. One of the first poems I ever wrote was the one about a trip to Trouville, called 'December 1991'. The title poem, 'We Travelled', about touring theatre in the late 1960s, is one of the most recent.

As for the essays, they are in more public territory. They cover a wide range of interests, from the photographer Lee Miller to the rapist Jimmy Savile, from Sarah Bernhardt to a former Archbishop of Canterbury, and from the essayist Joan Didion to the painter Patrick Caulfield. I think of them as palate-cleansers. Some of them make me feel very passionately indeed. An idealised description of my dream theatre ('The Playhouse') represents the sum of any wisdom I've acquired about how the best plays should best be allowed to breathe. 'A Twenty-First-Century Lexicon' is born of frustration. Few critics seem bothered that the way art is discussed is no longer adequate to the interesting directions art is taking. And an attempt to expose the contradictions in modern Conservatism ('In the Oxford Madrasa'), asking how anyone imagines they can have a free market without free movement of labour, was written some time before Brexit proved that, in spite of the lecture's guarded reception in Oxford, I may well have been on to something. When, in 2016, I first argued that modern Conservatism made no sense, the people David Cameron called 'the effing Tories' were in their pomp, and the audience was pretty dismissive. But now Toryism is in deep philosophical trouble, and any honest Tory privately admits it.

On most subjects in this book, however, I admit my own helplessness. I can rage all I like but nobody's taking any notice. I still see Tony Blair referred to all the time as an insincere salesman who believed in nothing. Plays on contemporary topics are still dismissed as dramatised journalism and therefore less profound than private plays. The name of Terence Rattigan is rarely mentioned without him being claimed as victim of something more than the usual vagaries of fashion. The 1970s provide social historians an inaccurate chance to proclaim a low point in modern British history. Journalists still get aggressive when actors cross their picket lines to give opinions on political and social subjects, about which some actors are as well qualified to speak as some journalists. People continue to claim that Anton Chekhov, the world's trickiest boyfriend, is best understood as a cool and objective writer. And as to lousy British war films . . . well, to this day, actors are playing balloon games on overloaded craft when scuttling from a hilariously implausible Dunkirk ('Sorry, old man, but we need to throw someone out'). And will Winston Churchill ever be talked out of his infuriating habit of going down the Tube in full slap and wig to consult with straphangers on the best way to win the war?

If the perspectives I offer remain unpopular, so be it. I can live with that, and have done for many years. In my defence, I cite the surrealist André Breton: 'It's wonderful to be so reviled at our age.'

DH
Lockdown London,
7 May 2021

ESSAYS

POPULIST? NOT VERY

In its daily more feverish attempts to push for the re-election of the sitting American president in the summer months of 2020, *The Times* took to referring to the incumbent as a populist. It was a strange word to use about Donald Trump. If there is such a thing, surely a populist has to be someone who has some appeal for an entire electorate. But Trump lost ground with those earning under $50,000 a year, was overwhelmingly unpopular with black voters by a factor of nine to one and commanded the support of only a minority of women. The young didn't like him. Hispanics preferred Joe Biden by a margin of 30 points. How could someone who repelled such significant sections of the voting public properly be called a populist?

Not for the first time, Rupert Murdoch was squirting his own brand of perfumed aerosol. The word, surely, was authoritarian.

Behind the careless use of the word 'populism' lies an assumption which runs both deep and ugly. In this world view, it is taken for granted that 'the people' – conveniently lumpen – are as mean and vindictive as the journalists who evoke them. In their writing, the white working class is always represented as aching for the swish of the guillotine. They're all driving around in white vans fighting for their own survival, sending donations to Migration Watch, carousing with Tommy Robinson and nursing early medieval views on crime and punishment. (None of them, naturally, work in hospitals, schools, care homes or any other essential service. None of them selflessly maintains the social fabric.) Only through the machinations of a liberal elite, it is implied, are these people denied what they truly want: for immigrants to die in the sea and for Western civilisation to purify itself of everything and everyone who contaminates it from outside.

The obvious trick behind this kind of polemic is to pretend that it's 'the people' who are the agents of reaction, and that, in a burst of disruptive energy, their thwarted desires are finally being acknowledged by rampant outsiders who have arrived fresh-faced in decadent capital cities like Washington DC, London, Budapest, Brasilia and Warsaw to outrage and defy the political establishment. Earlier this year, the one-time Conservative Anne Applebaum published a beautifully written and important book, *The Twilight of Democracy*, to kill this ridiculous narrative. She wrote of how many friends she had lost by refusing to surrender to the fashionable trend of pretending to be hard done by when you're on top. But she went on to ask the far more important question arising: why is the right wing, in Europe, in the UK, in India and in the US, moving so much further to the right?

Applebaum had lived in Eastern Europe before the fall of the Berlin Wall, so she brought an interesting perspective. She knew a little bit about collaboration by intellectuals inside corrupt regimes. She was horrified to see something of the same mentality developing in the West. Why were so many writers, editors and politicians ready to collude with known liars? Why had they abandoned their faith in reason and democracy, in order to offer unquestioning support to leaders like Donald Trump, Boris Johnson and Viktor Orbán, whom they knew to have a long record of almost never telling the truth? Why did they no longer trust that their own point of view might prevail through argument? Why were they frightened to disown malpractice on their own side? And why were they closing their eyes to the behaviour of leaders who were more suited to crashing round in the china shop than they were to restocking it?

Why, in other words, had the right abandoned its values?

While living in Poland in the 1980s, Applebaum had admired fellow anti-Communists. She had seen Conservatism in the UK and Republicanism in the US as philosophies which brought freedom. But now, in the twenty-first century, she could not understand the turn they had taken into what she felt to be despair. She had lost her affinity with a ruling class which had given up. She knew from first-hand experience that the responsibility for the impending chaos of Brexit, and all the nostalgia it was engendering, did not lie with an abandoned section of the electorate who were said to know no better. She could see that the white working class was being paraded as disingenuous cover for where the real responsibility lay: among the very people who had once been her colleagues.

It did not need Applebaum to point out that the people who were desperate to pull Britain away from its geographical moorings were as likely to be found in Knightsbridge as in Hartlepool. The leader of the UK Independence Party, Nigel Farage, who put the fear of God into the Conservative Party, was a stockbroker. His principal cheerleaders were press owners, paid-up members of an elite who all lived abroad: Rupert Murdoch, Lord Rothermere and the Barclay Brothers. The Conservative benches were stocked with entitled parliamentary opportunists who were well placed to survive turbulence. Again, their representative and, later, leader was an old Etonian, Boris Johnson. Just a handful of years earlier, before he morphed into yet another populist who mislaid his popularity, Johnson had been cheerfully pro-EU.

You may want to argue that so-called popular movements have always been led by characters from smart backgrounds. The British fascist leader of the 1930s, Oswald Mosley – Roderick Spode in P. G. Wodehouse's comic fiction – was a product of Winchester and Sandhurst, and newsreel shows him speaking to his ranks of anti-Semitic thugs in tones which sound absurdly posh to modern ears. Donald Trump, the great disrupter in the US, inherited a fortune from his father, which, by some calculations, would today be far greater if he had simply left it in the bank. But, even by historic standards, the Brexit movement does seem peculiarly lordly, depending on a generation of privileged journalists, politicians and financiers who wanted to kick away the European ladder on which they themselves had climbed. A bunch of Etonian politicians had benefited personally from social advances achieved by the liberal left. Not for them the untrendy prejudices of Section 28! But never once did they stop to acknowledge that it was their opponents who had secured them their new freedoms of lifestyle.

Meanwhile, Trump's parallel electoral tactic in the United States was to dispel the notion of shame. That ambition defined his project and was at the heart of his huge and stubborn appeal.

Trump promised to take the embarrassment out of people's own worst feelings. And by 'people' he didn't just mean the working class. Far from it. The well-to-do were to be given a free pass as well. Before Trump, the common pieties of public life had meant that any elector who had sexist or racist feelings, or who wanted always to insist on their own needs over the needs of others, might have felt vaguely rebuked by notions of good and bad. A scent of disapproval would have reached them from the religious and non-religious institutions which were there to help suggest social norms. But, under Trump, all bets were off. People of all backgrounds, super-rich and dirt poor, were given permission to feel whatever they damn well pleased by a president who proclaimed, 'Look at me, I'm never ashamed. I'm never contrite. Why should you be?'

All revolutions, whether of the right or the left, are powered by grievance. But the important question is always whether the grievance is real or concocted. In June 1975, I voted against Britain joining the Common Market on the usual leftist grounds that it was a capitalist cartel, and therefore a conspiracy against the poor. However, as the years went by, I began to see great advantages in belonging to a grouping in which most of the population were citizens, not subjects. It made a difference to the tone of debate. Because Britain, and England in particular, still took pride in a long-suffering culture eager to fall back on conservatism of all kinds, it was positive for us to join a club which led reluctant British governments towards a welcome emphasis on women's rights, workers' rights, consumer standards, equality, freedom and the rule of law. It was refreshing for our politics to have input from foreign politicians who seemed to have a scale and a vision ours lacked. We were in a group with a number of countries which were better governed than we were, and with a more urgent and accurate sense of history. European leaders such as Angela Merkel or François Mitterrand seemed like large figures, not least because they saw the future and weren't frightened of it.

Two aspects of European behaviour turned out to be attractive to any reluctant joiner like me. First, it was reassuring at a time when American foreign policy was getting daily crazier to be part, in letter if not in spirit, of an organisation which was neither craven towards, nor beholden to, the US. The EU acted as a counterbalance of sanity, particularly when, in the last century, American presidents were condoning illegality in Central America or the Middle East. During the build-up to the invasion of Iraq it was noticeable that, although the EU was not able to shake Tony Blair out of his school-prefect relationship with his headmaster, George W. Bush, the sanest voices of dissent came from countries to the south of us. France, in particular, spoke nothing but sense. If, as we believe, countless numbers of Iraqis have been killed by the consequences of the Anglo-American intervention, it ought to have been possible for us to be able to look across gratefully to well-meaning allies who were innocent of the damage and who were smart enough to foresee it. But rather than thanking them for warning against our foolishness, it is as if we are, through Brexit, intent on punishing our friends for being right.

The second unifying factor in Europe was a belief in multiculturalism. I had been brought up in an all-white seaside town in the 1950s, so I could see no downside to the tremendous vitality brought to large cities by immigration, at first from the West Indies, later from Africa. New arrivals cheered the country up, and did a lot to make it less smug and introspective. Later, when waves of refugees took to small boats in the Mediterranean, it was the Greeks, the Italians and the Germans who behaved heroically, doing their best by people whose only crime was to be born in places torn apart by invasion or by civil war. But, to our shame in the UK, it had in the interval become necessary to the overriding Brexit cause to insist, against all evidence, that multiculturalism had failed and that 'taking back control' must mean the same thing as closing down our borders. (This in spite of the fact that we were told at the same time that we needed to be part of something called the free market.)

Any Briton who has lived through the four years following the Brexit referendum and watched executive power being used to bypass Parliament and yielded without conscience to un-elected advisers in Downing Street will know just how hollow the promise to take back control has turned out to be. Was there no reason for it but spite? When I was young, there was a very funny column printed under the pseudonym of Peter Simple. It was whimsical regressive fantasy in the old *Daily Telegraph*, full of attacks on motoring and housing estates. Peter Simple extolled an England peopled by sheep, aristocracy and peasants, and unspoilt by psychology, materialism or the weakening of the class system. When he railed against psycho-analysts in Hampstead, the dog whistle was at full screech. But in an interview with the column's author, Michael Wharton, in the 1970s, he complained bitterly that, since his days at Oxford, it had always been assumed that such feudal attitudes must be a form of camp. It was amusing, of course, to want to take Britain back to the eighteenth century. It made good copy. But surely he couldn't possibly have meant it?

Something of the same disbelief arises when we look with any serious attention at the arguments of populists all over the world, who are as outraged as Peter Simple that onlookers think they're kidding. Is there a single person in the UK who today believes our country will be more prosperous outside the EU? Is there anyone in the US who believes that the building of a wall on the southern border will stop illegal immigration? Is there a single person in Brazil who thinks that it's wise to take no account either of science or medicine when dealing with a lethal pandemic? Does any woman believe Andrzej Duda in Poland is banning abortion for anything but the most cynical of electoral reasons? And is there anyone in India who doesn't know that Narendra Modi's citizenship law was anti-Muslim in intention and racist in execution?

Applebaum believes that Western countries are pulling out of democracy in a kind of intellectual funk, but surely these examples suggest that what we're pulling out of is modernity. Anyone with half a brain can see that in the twenty-first century the most urgent and most profound question will be how the 7 billion people in the world who are poor will be able to share a degree of opportunity with the billion who are rich. Boris Johnson's response is to put his head down and write books about Winston Churchill.

Again, one of the bleakest features of my adolescence in the 1960s was the ridiculous disparity between Britain's claims to global status and the reality of its condition. Harold Macmillan was rash enough to say that Britain was in an alliance with the US which resembled that of the Greeks with the Romans. We'd do the thinking, they'd do the enforcing. It became clear at the time that even if you could dismantle at least some parts of an empire at unexpected speed, dismantling the imperial thinking that went with it was going to take much longer. In the twentieth century, British institutions continued to behave as if they were powerful and unique long after they had ceased to be either. I had never thought that in the twenty-first century such grandiosity and stupidity would return. I thought the empire was dead. But the rhetoricians of Brexit chose, not purely for tactical reasons but because some of them actually believed it, to revive the convenient idea of British exceptionalism. Their loathing for progress could be deodorised only if they refloated the notion that Britain was different.

It's a challenge for any disruptive movement to maintain the energy of their grievance when they've achieved what they wanted. In 2021, this is the dilemma which faces populists all over the world. In many countries, self-styled outsiders have taken their turn at the heart of establishments from which they claimed to be excluded, and it gets harder to go on saying that everything is rigged in a terrible conspiracy against them. Trump, like Thatcher, passed his time as leader railing against his own administration, and even propagated the myth of a deep state which stole the election from him. But nothing could hide the fact that he had been the person in power. If he didn't like the weather, sorry, it was he who had made it. Trump was left, at the end, in the same position as Mao Zedong during the Cultural Revolution, deliberately inciting disorder in the form of an insurrection against the country he led and the institutions over which he governed. And in the UK, a similar loss of comforting paranoia continues to confound Brexiteers. They won. They have control. The government is led by one of their own. What happens is their fault, and nobody else's. If the United Kingdom does, as a result of Brexit, fracture either in Ireland or Scotland, if the economy falters, if the departure has already turned out more costly and disruptive than they predicted, they have no one to blame but themselves.

No wonder, therefore, that our friends, the would-be populists, are suddenly bereft. They must use all their ingenuity to summon up ever wilder grievances to power their motivating sense of injury. If overdogs are to go on pretending to be underdogs, they must dream up demands as impossibilist as possible. The first of these demands, outlined above, is suitably unlikely. Modern Britain must return to the 1950s. But the second demand is more sinister. The reason repeatedly advanced to explain the failure of the populists' endeavours to deliver paradise has been that although the priorities of the government are right wing, the underlying culture still is not.

It is in this context, created by the urgent desire to shift blame, that sustained and irrational attacks on the BBC and on the universities can best be understood. When Michael Gove says he is sick of experts, what he means is that he is sick of facts. In order to represent Britain as a hell of excess tolerance, which needs shaking up and made more verbally violent, it is vital for the Brexit victors to pretend that its broadcast media are biased, its civil servants are useless, and its teaching anti-imperialist. (If they thought they could get away with it, they would throw in their contempt for the NHS: only the NHS's universal popularity during Covid silences them.) When writers from the *Spectator* form a Free Speech Union, its aim is not, as you might hope, to expand the range and quality of public expression by attacking the ruthless no-platforming of non-conformists in the *Daily Mail*, the *Daily Telegraph*, the *Sunday Times*, the *Sun* and *The Times*. Nor is its interest in addressing the covert problems of censorship caused by minorities being under-represented in the mainstream. No, its purpose is to concentrate its efforts exclusively on protecting the right to give offence.

As someone who has spent the last fifty years writing, I, too, care about giving offence. It's vital. Whether doing it intentionally or unintentionally, I could hardly have worked without it. Nor would I ever forgo the chance to write about any culture or race or class I choose, trusting that I will be held to account by the far better-informed people I write about. As Cate Blanchett said, if she's not to be allowed to act people different from herself, she doesn't want to act. But it's precisely because these freedoms are so essential to me that I don't want to see them weaponised in a tedious culture war, waged for no honest reason except to divert attention from far deeper political failures.

This is at the heart of the problem for populists everywhere. They are not actually very popular any more. Yes, there are individuals within the electorate who feel fenced in by what they see as political correctness. But a far greater number of people believe that in our daily dealings with others, whatever their beliefs, we should show a degree of common courtesy, which corresponds to how we ourselves would wish to be treated. Yes, there are people in Bristol who would prefer the statues of slave-owners to be removed by the city council, and not toppled by students. But they are as nothing to the number of people in Bristol who are horrified by the slave trade in the first place. Yes, there are people in the United States who would like to see fewer immigrants from Mexico, but if the price of their exclusion is to be the separation of parents and children, they are not sure they want to pay that price. Yes, there is indeed in Britain an industrial working class that has been viciously hard done by in the shift from manufacturing and the years of public squalor and austerity. But polls show that they are already beginning to regret being talked into believing that their neglect ever had much to do with Brussels.

Applebaum believes that the answer to the question 'Why is the right moving so far right?' is philosophical. I believe it's tactical. There's nowhere else to go. For a right wing that is failing to deliver either the freedom or the prosperity they promised, the only possible route is towards the fantasy that they are being frustrated by hostile powers stronger than them. That's the alibi, that's the excuse. If only it were true.

(2021)

THE PLAYHOUSE

In 1946, George Orwell wrote his last essay for the *Evening Standard*. He described an imaginary pub, the Moon Under Water, where the music was quiet enough for conversation, the bar staff knew all the customers' names and you could always get a cut off the joint and a jam roll for three shillings.

For my whole life, I have dreamt of having my plays done at a theatre which, sadly, exists only in my mind, although the important elements of it, happily, exist in many.

Location

The ideal theatre – let's call it the Playhouse – will not be in the centre of London. It will be in a place where people actually live. That means either a regional city or a residential district in the capital. From 1957, Roger Planchon's exemplary Théâtre National Populaire thrived in Villeurbanne, a working-class suburb of Lyon, where, offering a programme rich with Racine and Molière, it rooted itself as deeply as Joan Littlewood's Theatre Workshop did in Stratford East. But when, in 2001, the Almeida followed Planchon's example by transplanting itself to the grottiest street in the old King's Cross, where audiences were regularly approached by prostitutes and criminals, somehow the mix of art and grime didn't graft.

Jonathan Meades is right when he argues that supporters of the arts like to exaggerate the effects of cultural regeneration.

The prosperity of the Almeida Theatre in Islington in the 1990s lifted the whole area. But it doesn't always work. As Meades says, in the two decades 'after the Guggenheim fell from the sky in Bilbao . . . the number of people unemployed or dependent on welfare has risen . . .' You can see something similar in my home town of Bexhill-on-Sea. The tasteful redevelopment of the De La Warr Pavilion in 2005, with its displays of cutting-edge conceptual art, has had little or no impact on the genteel charity-shop poverty of the streets around it. But it's impossible to shake the idea that you can't call anything a city unless it has a railway station, a bookshop, a post office, and a working theatre. If you travel across the US through countless towns where the only bookshops are either pornographic or religious, and where there is absolutely nothing in between, you will find yourself missing what spoilt metropolitans take for granted: mainstream culture.

Playing Space

The Minerva in Chichester is one of the best-designed theatres in the UK, because it has a huge playing space for epic plays, and yet the audience's experience is intimate. But fine as it is, it's still a black box, and very few black boxes carry history. They wipe themselves clean with each production. A theatre is partly memory, the residue of the greatness that's passed through. Ingmar Bergman called the older ones 'Stradivarius violins'. If you are my age, whenever you go to Aldwych Theatre, you will be moved to remember Paul Scofield playing King Lear, or Peggy Ashcroft playing Queen Margaret. It's where you saw Anna Magnani and Jean-Louis Barrault. At the Royal Court, you are in a space where

Caryl Churchill, John Osborne, Andrea Dunbar and Athol Fugard offered their most original work. In St Petersburg, it's impossible to visit the Alexandrinsky without being awed at the thought that you are sitting where *The Seagull* was first seen.

Certain theatres elevate plays, just by their atmosphere. In the late 1960s a brilliant group of young people including Jenny Harris and Ruth Marks commandeered a Victorian schoolroom up a side alley not far from the seafront to present a spontaneous slate of anarchist and communist plays. It seated only 80 people, and I never saw a show at the Brighton Combination which I didn't enjoy. But atmosphere is very hard to recreate. Clearly the Brooklyn Academy aspired, in its Majestic auditorium, to transport the magic of Peter Brook's Paris Bouffes du Nord for the transatlantic premiere of *The Mahabharata* in New York in 1988. But however assiduously they scraped the paint off the proscenium, and however rakishly they degraded the naked brickwork, the chichi effect was, and remains, disastrous. Nothing is worse than fake authenticity.

The danger of magical spaces is that plays may fall far short of expectations. Recently, I sat through a pretentious flop at the Royal Court thinking a flop in that beautiful house must be the most lowering experience any audience anywhere can have.

Size

This is difficult. People brought up in a world of film and television expect to be close to the action. They expect to be able to hear every word, and see every gesture. Rightly, they resent the class structures of playhouses built with differing perspectives at different prices. But a playwright needs to live. Unfortunately, you may be well known for your prestigious achievements in tiny studio theatres while also being stony broke. That may be one of the reasons some dramatists move too quickly to television. If, like Jez Butterworth, you have the skill and energy to write a play which reaches to the hearts of eight hundred people at once, the complex response of a large audience enriches the experience. A big house is like a field of wheat.

Policy

The primary purpose of the Playhouse will be to do new plays, and these plays will both represent and reflect the society they are performed in. There will be no need for gender or racial quotas, either on stage or off, because, by definition, if the artistic director follows this governing policy, everything good will follow. More than half the plays will be by women, women will gloriously people the stage, and the vibrant multiculturalism of the society we inhabit will be in front of you in its variety and abundance. Recently, the director of the Intiman Theatre in Seattle said that theatres needed to celebrate 'people standing in their own identities'. What a grisly idea! I feel the exact opposite. Theatres need to represent people reaching out across each other's identities.

The artistic director will be under thirty, because only the young can regenerate the form. The less contaminated he or she is by what is already thought to be good the better. But, best case, she will want a sprinkling of classics – Schiller, Ibsen, O'Neill – so that new plays may be seen in the context of old, with the aim of both paying tribute to a tradition and advancing it. When a production is of lasting value it will enter the repertory. In the

UK, we are amazingly careless with our best productions. They should not be thrown away so lightly. Andrew Scott will play Hamlet at the Playhouse annually for a season. Lesley Sharp will reprise her Helen in *A Taste of Honey*. Can someone call Linda Bassett, please, about doing Barney Norris's *Visitors* again?

Staffing

Everyone in the theatre will work towards what happens onstage. What's more, they will often attend it. There is no artistic sight more depressing in London than the flow of staff leaving the National Theatre at 6 p.m. Many theatre organisations are overfull with people who have nothing to do with putting on plays. Many are forced into something thankless called development, trying to get indifferent private sponsors to perform the state's duties. The National has roughly twice as many employees as it had when it opened in 1976 in order to do fewer productions. Many of them never look up from their desks. They are forced to stare all day at computers, ticking boxes on forms sent to them by the Arts Council. At the Playhouse, computers will be centrally shut down at 4.30 p.m., so everyone can turn their attention to the night's work.

In his book *A Sense of Direction*, the one-time director of the Royal Court, Bill Gaskill, tells of sitting one afternoon, alone and thoughtful, in the dress circle of the theatre while Elsie, the cleaning lady, worked below. When an actor burst into the stalls, Elsie hushed him with the words, 'You have to be quiet. Tonight's a very important opening for Bill.' It was a perfect example of a theatre where everyone, including the cleaner, was committed and working to one purpose. But commitment should work both ways. That's why Ariane Mnouchkine, the director of the Théâtre du Soleil, was often found tearing tickets as the audience came in to the Cartoucherie in Paris. The artistic director of the Playhouse will work alongside the many drama students who become ushers in order to watch and learn from great actors every night.

The State

In the late 1980s, Peter Hall said, 'The great experiment is over.' Since he was born in 1930, Hall said, he had seen the birth of the welfare state, and of the notion that government was responsible for the decent standard of life of its citizens. If the state was a benign enabler, it would cheerfully enable art, health and education. This belief was uncontested by all political parties for a forty-year consensus, which, in theatre, saw both company and repertory flourish, because they were affordable. Only with the arrival of the Thatcherites did representatives of the state – themselves lavishly rewarded by the state; Thatcher, after all, was content to live off public money – begin to deny their responsibilities. By starving theatre of funds, they forced the subsidised sector to adopt the values of the commercial. As Peter Gill wrote, *Look Back in Anger* in 1956 was undoubtedly the most influential event in post-war theatre. But the second most influential was the commercial investment in the RSC's musical production of *Les Misérables* in 1985. It turned subsidised theatre from a culture with its own values into a shouty seedbed with an eye on the main chance.

The Playhouse will be subsidised by the state alone.

Touring

In return for this largesse, the Playhouse will tour, and tour often. The abandonment of touring by our best-funded companies is a major scandal, which goes unremarked year after year. The argument that it is elitist to take metropolitan productions to the regions and that the regions are better off making their own work is phooey. The two should coexist, and should cross on the motorway. *The Ferryman*, *Consent*, *Ink* and *Mosquitoes* should all be out on the road right now, so the whole country can see them. The work of Newcastle Live and Theatre Clwyd should be regularly coming to town. Because cinema streaming reaches good audiences at good prices, it will feature strongly. But it will be used as an addition to, not a substitute for, large- and small-scale touring.

School

In an annexe of the Playhouse, beside the canal, will be a small school, where, in addition to acting, students will be taught theatre's vital skills – stage management, scene painting, costume design – by the same people who work in the Playhouse. Apprentices and practitioners will mix freely. The courses will not be academic; they will be practical. The history of theatre will be taught, but lightly – to inform the students, not to examine them. The recent push to devitalise drama schools by turning them into degree-course theory-of-performance academies has been disastrous.

Playwrights

Briefly, in the 1990s, an office was designated at the National Theatre called the Writers' Room where a number of dramatists all worked on their current projects. Howard Brenton, Tony Harrison and Tony Kushner would all arrive at 10 a.m. and take the milk bottles in. For once, writers were a genuine part of the life of the theatre, not just visitors to rehearsals. Needless to say, our office eventually got taken away for some more bureaucratic purpose. But while it lasted, it was heaven. The Playhouse will have a writers' room.

Workshops and Readings

All plays submitted will be read. This will be guaranteed. But out-loud readings will be rare, and only with the writer's consent. A young playwright complained to me recently that she had been commissioned to write a play for a well-known address. When she finished it, the artistic director said it needed a workshop. The dramatist thought it didn't. The writer's wishes were overruled and the workshop went ahead, evidence of nothing but the management's bad faith. In some theatres, workshops and readings are deployed as stalling devices by artistic directors who pretend they are interested in new plays, but who use uncertainty and hesitation in staging them as a means of extolling and abusing their power. At the Playhouse workshops and readings will never be designed as hurdles a writer has to jump. In short, there will be genuine equality between actor, writer and director.

Actors

Certain actors will be associated with the Playhouse. Audiences have lost one of the pleasures of theatregoing – the link between particular houses and particular actors. You can rarely expect at any current venue to see the progress and versatility of a single actor. A new generation of enlightened agents will explain to their clients that a big theatre success is more likely to fulfil their dream of Hollywood stardom than playing fifth banana in a new soap.

Audience

There will be no targeting of individual productions towards individual ethnicities or age groups. Such policies are demeaning, and misunderstand the nature of art. Black people go to Picasso shows and white people go to see Basquiat. *Angels in America* plays as powerfully to straight people as it does to gay. When Ralph Fiennes played *The Master Builder*, a white play by a white nineteenth-century playwright, the Old Vic was packed to the rafters with a diverse audience because everyone, whatever their race, whatever their age and whatever their gender, wanted to see a great actor command a great role. At the Southwark Playhouse, Sharon D. Clarke used the Cy Coleman musical, *The Life*, to rock every nationality known to humanity. At the Playhouse, people will go to the work because it's good, not because it's ingratiating.

Safe Space

In my youth, directors were often monsters and bullies. Choreographers and conductors were worse. They shouted and screamed at the people who did the job. It was tolerated. But in today's theatre culture, directors like Lindsay Anderson and choreographers like Jerome Robbins would rarely be seen in the building, because they would always be on away-days, sitting anger-management courses. In matters personal, the Playhouse will not need enforcement rules because respect for actors and employees would be a given. However, in matters artistic, the space will be extremely unsafe.

Site-Specific

If a director can produce a very strong argument, she or he will be allowed to present a play away from the Playhouse. But this will not happen often. When Patrice Chéreau staged *In the Solitude of the Cotton Fields* in a disused factory outside Paris, the dust and the light made Bernard-Marie Koltès's text sparkle. Jerzy Grotowski's use of an empty film studio for Stanisław Wyspiański's play *Akropolis* added to the desolation of that extraordinary evocation of the concentration camps. But gimmicky stagings inside gasholders or behind supermarkets will be discouraged. There are sound democratic reasons for theatre taking place in spaces where everyone can see, hear, think and feel together.

Critics

Because they exist to serve the audience, critics will be outsiders, not panting wannabe insiders. They will know as much about the outside world as they do about theatre. The primary context for judging the play will be real life. They will resist the facile temptation to give dramatists, directors and actors a diagnostic report on their status within the fluctuations of their own art form. Critics will review plays, not reputations. Above all, they will be able to write English. Those critics who cannot construct a halfway readable sentence in their native language will not be invited to review work at the Playhouse.

Restaurants and Bars

It's an iron rule that all theatre restaurants are terrible. A rare exception was at the Liverpool Everyman in the 1970s, where the food was cheap, plentiful and delicious – and, crucially, the atmosphere was informal. The cast all ate there. The hamburgers at the King's Head were once legendary. But some theatres don't attempt catering. At the Bouffes du Nord in Paris, where Peter Brook did some of his greatest work, there were only occasional croissants, and hard-boiled eggs to dip in salt. It didn't matter because the bar was used by the actors. It's the mix of actors and spectators which brings a theatre bar to life. The conversations that follow are far more enjoyable and informative than any organised Q&A. The best pick-up spot was always at the Traverse when it was in the Grassmarket in Edinburgh in the 1970s. People keep saying theatre should change your life. Well, many lives were changed – at least for a night – in that bar.

Effect

The effect of the Playhouse will be to cheer everyone up. No, it will not save lives, like a great hospital. But it will restore spirits, like a great sunset. Most of all, it will be genuinely collaborative, proving to the country that things we do together have a quality all of their own. Most of all, it will express a trust in theatre itself as a unique form which does something profound no other form can. The Playhouse will not suck up to other disciplines in a desperate attempt to make itself trendy. It will use dance and music judiciously, as a way of reinforcing its own effects, but never to obliterate word and image. Nor will it ever allow itself to be reduced to a gibbering variation on galleried performance art. There will be no self-referential evenings of angst which neurotically question the value and nature of the form. It will be staffed by people who have confidence in that form, who love it, and who are, in the experience of their own lives, benefiting immeasurably from its special power.

(2017)

DIRECTORS' THEATRE

When I first started working in the late 1960s, three writers, Samuel Beckett, John Osborne and Harold Pinter, were the leading names in the British theatre. But alongside them there existed two influential directors, both of whom belong in any history of their chosen art form. At Stratford East, Joan Littlewood and, at the Royal Shakespeare Company, Peter Brook both used dramatists in ways which were non-traditional. Littlewood had a strong hand in plays by Shelagh Delaney and Brendan Behan to a point where scholars have trouble disentangling their individual contributions. Things went further when the writer was encouraged to be in the rehearsal room primarily to serve the director's purpose.

From this new arrangement came work like Littlewood's *Oh, What a Lovely War!*, which integrated song, technology, action, character, history, improvisation and political analysis to an unprecedented degree. A fierce argument about billing followed the opening, with misleading posters having to be repasted by negotiation. Brook, once happy to direct writers like John Whiting and Friedrich Dürrenmatt, moved on from doing things which were clearly plays to things which were better described as shows. Brook insisted there was no such thing as just 'doing the play' and even moved from doing whole plays by Shakespeare to offering inspired fragments.

As someone who was first excited to work in the theatre by Brook's and Littlewood's contrasting forms of idealism, I have no problem with the idea of Directors' Theatre. It's because I admired it so much in the 1960s that I am shocked at how low its prevailing standards have become, and how lazy its tropes. When Stephen Daldry, the greatest of Joan Littlewood's descendants, was asked what was the weakest element in British theatre, he replied 'Us' – meaning directors. A generation of genuine innovators – Giorgio Strehler, Ingmar Bergman, Roger Planchon – has largely been succeeded by a generation content to inherit.

A good proportion of fashionable work is copied straight from Page One of the Peter Brook playbook. When Brook first deployed them, white sets, abstract blocking, video screens, monsoons of blood, collapsing walls, needless underscoring, half-light, revolving angles of view, deeply sloping ramps, and actors squirming like beached mammals in foams and liquids were all startling. Today they have become the clichés of first resort, which are slapped on at random intervals to send out avant-garde signals of category. Second-hand images are applied from outside, rather than allowed to grow from in-.

What is most dismaying is how openly misogynist this varnish has become. It always seems to be women who are compelled to crawl on all fours round the stage, on the ridiculous grounds that smearing female underwear with blood or shit represents a critique of patriarchy. The audience receives the familiar images of degradation as nothing but apolitical nihilism. The opera houses of Europe are overrun with leatherclad whores and pimps, cracking whips or bare-arsed. The most impassioned revolt against the global spread of European theatre practice has come not from playwrights, but from actors, and particularly female actors. Many women tell you how weary they are of being robbed of their own imaginations and treated like puppets by directors using parade-ground techniques to sidestep far more profound questions about narrative and psychology.

Since the Second World War, the director has always been a powerful figure, because directors run subsidised theatres and therefore choose the plays. They're the producers. Even the Royal Court Theatre, which in its heyday many years ago was regarded as the ultimate playwrights' theatre, was run exclusively by directors. The plays which went on were not necessarily the best. They were the ones the directors wanted to direct. Today, the Royal Court's silence on the autonomy and primacy of the individual writer is crushing, and betrays that theatre's reason for existing. On the current list of artistic associates at the National Theatre, you will find the names of a sound designer, a lighting designer and an actor. You will not find a working playwright.

This denial of the dramatist's standing chimes with a post-modernist notion that an existing play is just a text with which the director may do whatever they choose. In his 1986 book *Subsequent Performances*, Jonathan Miller argued that because you could never discover an author's intentions you were free to ignore them. Running with that argument, directors have since turned plays into little more than lumps of raw material to be retro-rigged by people who lack the skill to initiate but who – more like critics than artists – have the skill to react. Hence the prevailing preference for adapting novels or old films, or indeed anything which has already succeeded in another medium. Shows made from other media can be re-engineered more easily with the one-size-fits-all expressionist toolkit.

Young directors, setting out in their twenties into what has become a hotly competed field, tell me they have felt compelled, against their better judgement, to throw in some gratuitous splashes, in order to attract attention. The beauties of genuine collaboration no longer draw the spotlight. As Arthur Miller put it, directors have taken not to directing the play, but to directing what the play reminds them of.

It will be sad if theatre throws away its unique advantage over other performing arts. When young playwrights ask me how writing for the stage compares with writing for the cinema, I point out that the crucial difference is not artistic but legal. When you write screenplays, you are a hired hand, offering a day's labour. The result may thereafter be jerked around without your consent by anyone who buys your work. But when you work in the theatre, you remain the owner of your own copyright. If the production does not represent a good-faith account of what you wrote, you have the contractual right to argue for your governing ideas or close the production down.

I have exercised this right only once – as it happens, in the Greek theatre at Epidaurus. Having chosen to present a play which sought to elucidate the reasons for the banking crisis of 2008, the director implied by getting his actors to perform as offensive halfwits that it was impossible to elucidate that crisis. *The Power of Yes* was manipulated to express the exact opposite of my own reason for writing it. An eight-nation tour had to be cancelled. Harold Pinter caused a scandal by exercising his legal right in Rome in 1973, when he attended the 35th performance of Luchino Visconti's production of *Tanto tempo fa* (*Old Times*) at the Teatro Argentina and closed it down. 'I did not write a play about two lesbians who caress each other continually. There is nothing in the text that indicates that the man and woman powder the naked breasts of the wife on stage. I did not write a scene about a man masturbating his wife.'

Today, everyone seems to believe that the dead are fair game. But, happily, it's still rare for a living dramatist to look at a production and say, 'This is not what I wrote.' Since I have been lucky enough twice to see Katie Mitchell's production of the George Benjamin–Martin Crimp opera *Written on Skin* in Vicki Mortimer's designs, I know we still have directors who can imagine brand-new images which are mysterious, germane and gorgeously suggestive. But the brute power structure of the industry, and fake populist politics – 'Hey, my view's as good as yours' – is pushing theatre in a direction where an individual's view of the world is no longer supreme, or supremely valued. Yes, your view is indeed as good as mine. I agree. But a work of art is not an opinion. It's a complete imagined world. Let's have a chance to hear each other first before we drown each other out. Let's value skill. Writers, like directors, like actors, do something no one else can do. Group-conceived shows too often reinforce the common wisdom. Writers like to defy it. If theatre is there purely to celebrate what you already believe, then company creation is fine. But if you want a challenge to what you believe, a playwright is indispensable.

An outsider may well not be surprised that, at a time of reactionary politics, art theory is taking a corresponding visceral lurch to the right. But my hope for darkening times is that theatre might not do the political authoritarians' work for them. That will mean plays, and plays by individuals, with specific meanings.

(2020)

31

A TWENTY-FIRST-CENTURY
LEXICON

Art

On an edition of *Start the Week* in the early 1990s, Norman Tebbit, one-time Chair of the Conservative Party, asked his fellow guests why a Rolls-Royce jet engine could not be regarded as a work of art. Understandably, his question sounded chippy. His boss, Margaret Thatcher, had never been popular with the majority of artists. Without having time to think, I replied by saying that although the jet engine was an object of exceptional skill and beauty, it was fashioned without any metaphorical intention. It was a thing whose only subject was itself. A work of art must be suggestive of something beyond. I have no idea if I was right.

Vocabulary

The standard vocabulary of art talk seems exhausted, geared for the wrong century. Most everyday arts writing strings together words which, like blackened teeth, have hollowed out with overuse. The terms which were current in the twentieth century no longer compute in the twenty-first, now that art is delivered and distributed differently. When so much is more easily available, at least at second hand, can anything any longer be described as 'cutting edge' or 'avant-garde'? 'Feminist' doesn't mean much except 'has a woman in it'. 'Conceptual' just means 'illustrating a familiar idea'. 'Diverse' means 'has a black actor in it'. 'Iconic' means 'has been around for a long time'. 'Expressionist' means 'shamelessly over-acted'. Does anyone believe that there are any longer people called 'bohemians'?

What does the word 'outsider' mean when it's deployed by every actor, artist, politician and dentist looking for a way to suggest they're not boring? The poor, the indigent and people who have arrived illegally still live outside Western societies. They're outsiders. But, truly, who else?

Radical

In politics, 'radical' was once a good left-wing word, but it has lately been appropriated by the right wing to suggest any challenge to the prevailing wisdom from whatever direction, but most commonly from the right.

Elitist

In culture, 'elitist' was once a good left-wing word used to attack cultural forms which were conceived to flatter the ruling class but it has lately been appropriated by the right wing to attack the very notion of culture itself. By this new definition, everyone who enjoys certain specialised cultural forms is elitist.

Culture

Seventy years ago, a group of writers including Raymond Williams and Richard Hoggart in their books *Culture and Society* and *The Uses of Literacy* expanded the idea of what culture might be. It wasn't the art which came out of drawing rooms from a privileged group at the top of society. It was the whole sum of what was going on at all economic and social levels. The feeling of the time, as manifested through art, came up from below.

In Raymond Williams' most famous assertion, 'Culture is ordinary.'

These working-class academics had particular hostility to haughty writers, handily represented by people like F. R. Leavis and the Bloomsbury Group, who shared a myth of a Britain destroyed by the Industrial Revolution, and who spoke of the masses as ignorant and the culture as dying. As Williams insisted, 'A dying culture, and ignorant masses, are not what I have known and see.'

Out of this same desire to look more widely and deeply in the 1950s came a new British cinema, pioneered by people like Karel Reisz and Jack Clayton; a new British theatre, pioneered in the regions and in London; and most importantly of all, in the 1960s, a new British music, inspired by black America. This music cheered everyone up when it blew fresh air through the stale chambers of high culture.

The impulse behind this widespread opening-out was decent and democratic. But in the 1980s the same impulse was appropriated by a group of right-wing militants who formalised their hostility to all things intellectual – and, more pressingly, their social distaste for intellectual types – by declaring that anything which smelt of the highbrow was, by definition, elitist.

Their mission was to elide the words 'popular' and 'good'.

Anything which was admired by large groups of people was superior to anything which was admired by small groups. Difficulty and pretension were the same thing. Newspapers began to favour charts showing how well a work of art was doing over lengthy examinations of what it might be saying. The salesroom correspondent had an importance denied to the art critic. The

New York Times began to report cinema box-office results, and, in British broadsheets, TV ratings were given prominence over TV reviews. Restaurant critics became top dogs.

This new movement found its home in a supplement of Rupert Murdoch's *Sunday Times*, which was wittily named Culture, in order to house a generation of writers who loathed culture and everything it was understood to represent. Its TV critic, A. A. Gill, even argued that the day of the individual writer was over, and that British TV could match the vitality of American only when it went over to the group-writing system which prevailed in writers' rooms in the US.

Historically, Gill could not have been more wrong.

Religion

'I didn't kill the enemy because the enemy wanted to listen to a concert in A minor while I preferred a concert in A major. I killed him because he took the bread away from our German families. I love a good film, a play, a book, I love art, but when I'm hungry the best film does not interest me.'

Adolf Eichmann's words challenge the impossible burden put on art in the twentieth century by the decline of religion. Eichmann was having none of it. Late-Victorian thinkers had argued that when God died people would turn to culture to do the heavy lifting previously achieved by belief. No matter if people were no longer awed by divinity, instead they could at least be awed by art. In the process, good behaviour would be encouraged.

As Terry Eagleton put it, 'Matthew Arnold's idea of culture is a gentrified form of Christianity.'

Tyrants like Hitler and Stalin picked up the challenge. They both held vehement views about art, and were able to ban or encourage art which they interpreted as hostile or friendly to their own political ideas. Hitler was rung by Winifred Wagner in 1933 and asked for his opinion on the possible décor for a new production of *Parsifal* at Bayreuth. (Winifred, a Hastings girl by birth, was in love with him.) Hitler was thrilled to be consulted as associate designer to an opera house, and threw his weight behind the idea that classic works must always be seen afresh in updated productions. It would be absurd, Hitler said, to go on doing *Parsifal* in the original designs. Just because Richard Wagner had seen things a particular way, that was no reason why each generation should not be free to reinterpret.

Three years later, in 1936 in the Soviet Union, a new opera, Shostakovich's *Lady Macbeth of Mtsensk*, incurred Stalin's anger. To Shostakovich's alarm, Stalin was seen to laugh derisively during the love scenes. The opera was then immediately attacked in *Pravda* as 'Muddle Instead of Music'. The composer was initially defiant – 'Even if they cut off both my hands and I have to hold the pen in my teeth, I shall still go on writing music' – and used religious imagery to describe the attacks: 'He who doubted was guilty of a crime against Stalin's regime, and the sinner could save himself only by repenting.' But he soon withdrew his Fourth Symphony, and accused himself of 'grandiosomania'. Shostakovich continued to suffer appallingly for years to come. The idea of art taking over the function of religion was not an unmixed blessing for the artist.

Architecture

In the last century, the religious notion of art was expressed architecturally. The Barbican, National Theatre and Southbank Centre in London and the Lincoln Center in New York were all built in the mid-twentieth to express separation. Like cathedrals, major arts centres stood alone and proud, and free of the traffic of commerce. They were sanctuaries for the soul, often in forbidding styles. But in the last fifty years these holy places have panicked at their own isolation and transformed themselves to look as much like the rest of the city as possible.

The Barbican Centre was once famous for its impenetrability. It was not meant for strangers. The idea was that only regular devotees would be able to find their way around. Everyone else could get lost. And did. Today, its off-brown pebbledash is bedecked with friendly signage.

The Southbank has also been rebooted as a party venue for countless merrymakers. On Thursday and Friday nights, tens of thousands stand on the terraces getting hammered, oblivious that, inside, orchestras continue to play music which requires astonishing levels of skill and virtuosity. Inside the walls of the National Theatre, Chekhov and Shakespeare are performed by actors who need to dedicate themselves to years of diligent practice and experience. But the foyers have been redecorated to look like airport duty-free shops and evoke commercial normality. Outside those same walls, in summertime, jugglers, singers and dancers are invited to do what more or less anyone can do after a pint and a day's rehearsal.

The people who jazz these buildings into non-specialness seem to be apologising for the almost superhuman degree of expertise required inside. They're embarrassed. They see any expression of highly developed creativity as being the enemy of the creativity which is in all of us, instead of being an aspect of its sublime expression. Inequality of skill is taken to be as offensive as inequality of opportunity and wealth. Special accomplishment, accepted in football, is treated as anti-democratic in art.

The river entrance to the National Film Theatre was shut for over a year. It has finally reopened. The only visible change is a new bar, which significantly resembles the one it replaces, only larger. New neon replaces old neon. The auditoria showing the films are untouched.

If the performing arts ever did have a spiritual mission, popular opinion today demands it be disguised.

Agitprop

This beautiful word has become a term of critical abuse, always linked with an adjective – 'crude' or 'predictable'. Too many fringe-theatre plays with capitalists in top hats and carrying swag marked with dollar signs took their toll. Shelley's 'The Mask of Anarchy' – 'I met Murder on the Way – / He had a mask like Castlereagh' – is pure agitprop, and all the more powerful for it.

Agitprop's recent transformation from good to bad is powered by the modern critical belief that artistic work is stronger when it represents all points of view. This is obvious nonsense. Would *The Diary of Anne Frank* be better for giving equal weight to both Nazi and Jew? Would *Paths of Glory* be improved by putting more energy behind the case for military executions? Or would *Ugetsu Monogatari* be more moving if we saw things from the rapists' angle? I don't think so. One of my favourite films is Kurosawa's *The Bad Sleep Well* (1960). Its ferocious attack on corruption in Japanese business circles after World War Two is far more one-sided and damning than anything ever seen in a British movie or TV film. But because it's by Kurosawa, nobody notices and nobody attacks it as agitprop.

Diversity

The argument for diversity in the arts does not rest, as opponents represent it, on social engineering. It is to improve the odds on great work. Limit the pool of people making art to one gender, one social class and one racial background and you limit the likelihood of it being first rate. Our educational system is so intermittent and flawed that large numbers of people do not think about becoming writers, dancers, musicians or painters. In the narrowness of the opportunities we offer, we have wasted the potential of thousands of artists. Everything we can possibly do to expand the number of people who feel that, with perseverance, they might have great art in them is worth doing. Our reasons should be selfish. We wish our favoured art forms to be greater.

Imagination

Bitter experience has taught me that the representation of women and ethnic minorities in film and theatre has not changed because of what has been happening inside those industries. It has changed because of what has been happening outwith. It's patronising to offer yet again the stale argument that excluded groups should be included because they have new stories to tell. That view implies that all art is necessarily, and solely, autobiographical. No creative person, of whatever background, wants to write exclusively from their own silo. Yes, of course, perspective is an element in creativity. But it's not the whole thing. There's more to creativity than the generic trigger 'as a woman' or 'as an African-American'. Great art is created as much from the imagination as from experience. It's the distinctive mix of the two which is exhilarating. Certainly, any ethnic group may want to bring forward stories of their own culture. The more, the better. But those same groups are entitled to reflect their own lives by analogy, not just recreate them from memory. Nobody can forbid minorities the right to invent stories of others. Syrians have a perfect right to write about Cuba. Cubans have a perfect right to write about Ascot races. The urgent, scandalous question is: why are they getting so little opportunity to do so?

Madness

In the twentieth century the mad were held to have unique access to the mysteries of the universe. Who believes that now? Who thinks drugs open the doorways of perception?

Method Acting

Method acting was a style of performance which was invented to celebrate outsiderism. Its signature was an inarticulacy which was intended to imply that the actor, almost always male, was good in bed.

Because the idea of the outsider is defunct, so is the method. Already, old Sean Penn films look more mannered and dated than old Rex Harrison films.

Cinema versus Television

The first casualty of streamed television drama on channels where you can watch the whole series at once is always said to be old-fashioned network drama. But that's not true. It's American independent cinema which has suffered more. Art-house cinema had always been dependent on mood, charm, social detail and accuracy. It has not been able to compete with narrative television, whose priorities are story, story and story. Mood has always been a signifier of highbrow, as has mumbling; narrative and clear speaking signifiers of low- and middlebrow.

Pauline Kael once claimed there was no such thing as a television film. In her view, it was a contradiction in terms. Thank God we have moved on since then, and the move towards larger reach and wider subject matter is, on the whole, invigorating. Few viewers will favour *Marriage Story* over *Chernobyl*. But there is a balance here between slow-cooked food and fast, which will one day be redressed. Tiny stories which thrive on nuance will be allowed back.

Learned versus Naive

In the introduction to his post-war anthology, *The New Poetry*, the critic Al Alvarez wrote of the gulf between two strands in British poetry. On one side was the romantic kind, an outpouring of personal feeling, as exemplified by Wordsworth. On the other was the learned or academic kind, tending, like

T. S. Eliot's, towards the evasion of feeling, and informed by a comprehensive knowledge of the history of the art form.

In one incarnation, the poet was a bard. In the other, a scholar.

In 1962, Alvarez hoped this gulf would be bridged in his lifetime. He would be disappointed to know that when a friend of mine recently published a book of poetry after a career spent doing something else, many people remarked on his 'courage'. Essentially, they wanted to warn him that modern poetry was so vexed and contentious a field that it was foolhardy to write poetry without knowing what state-of-the-art thinking ruled was good or bad.

This view of art as a competition which may be entered only by experts is profoundly depressing. At its worst it's represented by Eliot's casual claim to Virginia Woolf that they were both as good as Keats because 'we're trying something harder'. Novels in the United States are written largely by people who teach novels. I attend an awful lot of plays written by playwrights who have all too clearly been to see an awful lot of plays. There are few romantics. But the new voice, the untutored voice, thrills me in a way no other can. Twice in 2018, reading new books by Sally Rooney and Rachel Kushner, I felt, 'Nobody else could have written this.' Both effortlessly bridge the gulf between the learned and the romantic.

Words

In the last lesson he gave to his students, the American poet James Dickey said that civilisation was being driven into suicide by the feeling that nothing matters very much. 'That is what is behind all the drugs and the alcoholism and suicide – insanity, wars, everything – a sense of non-consequence.' He argued that poets had to be free from that feeling precisely because they were creators – secondary creators, naturally, but still creators. 'For the poet everything matters, and it matters a lot. That is where we work. Once you are there, you are hooked. If you are a real poet, you are hooked more deeply than any narcotics addict possibly could be on heroin. You are hooked on something which is life-giving rather than destructive.'

If Dickey was right, people in the new century are going to need art more than ever. Theorists who feared that books, paintings and plays would face extinction have discovered instead that these forms are prospering and valued because they offer relief from the casual screen. New things are happening which render categories of high- and lowbrow meaningless. But the language in which the arts are discussed seems not to have caught up.

It was Donald Trump, that most exhausting of rhetoricians, who observed, 'I know words. I have the best words.' The words used to talk about art right now are as anachronistic and formulaic as the ex-president's. The ideas have moved on, but the language to describe those ideas hasn't. Sixty years ago, Kenneth Tynan, the most incisive theatre reviewer of my lifetime, wanted to give up being a critic because he couldn't stand the word 'relevant' any more. Who can blame him? But it's worse today. Art's running ahead, the way it's discussed is running far, far behind.

(2018)

43

IN THE OXFORD MADRASA

A lecture given at Trinity College, Oxford, on 3 March 2016, in memory of Richard Hillary, the fighter pilot who died at twenty-three, having written The Last Enemy, *about the Battle of Britain*

It's daunting for me to be invited into Oxford to speak, since it's both a town and a university of which I've had almost no experience. Occasionally, since the 1950s, whenever prime ministers have shown either unusual stupidity or unusual ignorance and I have asked the question, 'Where on earth was he or she educated?', the answer has invariably been 'Oxford'. What did they read? Usually PPE (Politics, Philosophy and Economics). If you regard Britain's period of adjustment after the revolt of its empire as calm and temperate, you will think of the adolescent playground of its leaders as benign. If you regard that same period as shameful and embarrassing, you will think of Oxford less well.

My most prolonged stay in town was just over forty years ago when I wrote a play called *Knuckle*, which tried out for two weeks at the Oxford Playhouse, before going on to open in the West End. It was my fourth full-length play, and it suffered a difficult birth. I was twenty-six. If only I had known it, its reception was to have a decisive and lasting effect on my life. *Knuckle* was produced at a time of bitter and fundamental industrial disputes, so the hotel I stayed in along from the theatre was subject to blackouts. It was February and it was freezing cold, and there were evenings when the hotel was lit by candles placed on the stairs and in your room.

Edward Heath, a Conservative prime minister, Balliol-educated, was about to announce an unwise election based around the question 'Who Runs Britain?' He was tired, he said, of the unions having too much power and he wanted to settle the arguments between government and workers once and for all. At the end of March, the electorate gave him a dusty answer – it's always a mistake to go to the people with a question they expect you to answer for yourself – but Heath hung on for a few undignified days in Downing Street, trying to cobble together a coalition against the people's wishes, before gracelessly accepting the inevitable. There was a camp aspect to his grumpiness which was irresistibly comic. Heath had lost and he wanted everyone else to be punished. Harold Wilson, the victor, once an Oxford don, quickly settled with the miners, and the lights came back on again.

You tend to remember such times.

In contrast, the twenty-first century announced its bumpy character from the start. The millennium was pretty soon marked by the destruction of the Twin Towers in New York, and then by the misappropriation of that event by opportunistic politicians in the West in order to launch a long-nurtured plan to invade Iraq – achieved (need I say?) with the collusion of an Oxford-educated British prime minister, a lawyer who, paradoxically, turned out to be willing to believe any old rubbish which suited his purposes, rather than stopping to weigh the evidence. The American government suspended

45

habeas corpus, abandoned the Geneva Convention, allowed its intelligence officers and its military personnel to engage in torture, while wiretapping its own citizens. A global financial crash, another unhappy invasion, this time of Libya, a ferocious civil war, much of it between at least two ruthless factions in Syria, a massive immigration crisis in Europe, the annexation of the Crimea and parts of Ukraine by the Russian Federation, the renewed bombing of Gaza, the brief renaissance and then the violent suppression of democracy in Egypt, terrorism in Paris and the collapse of the entire Greek economy have kept the 24-hour news channels ticking over nicely. Seldom in my lifetime – I missed Hitler by two years – has there been so much unwelcome news.

The past is comparatively safe, next to the present, because we know how at least one of them turns out. Or do we? One of my purposes in last year publishing a memoir, *The Blue Touch Paper*, which describes my growing up and my beginnings as a writer, was to reclaim the 1970s from the image which politicians of one fierce bent have imposed with the help of compliant historians. A frightening number of lazy books portray that decade as deadlocked and barren. The familiar version of our island story is that we all spent the 1970s in industrial chaos, with successive governments failing to confront the overbearing unions, until Margaret Thatcher arrived and set about deregulating markets, privatising public assets and encouraging citizens to work only for ourselves and our own self-interest.

This, we have been told over three decades of sustained propaganda, was wholly to the good. The country we live in today with all its crazy excesses of inequality and flagrant immorality in the workplace – bosses in large firms averaging 160 times the salaries of their worst-off employees – is said to be far superior to how it was in the days when labour still held management in some kind of check. According to their watchdog, energy companies overcharge customers by £1.2 billion a year, while water companies, according to MPs, have overcharged by a mere billion pounds in the last five years. Privatised monopolies are not – perish the thought! – vicious cartels ripping out profits and providing lousy service to their furious customers. No, they are bracing expressions of vigour and initiative, even when they strangle the market to a point where competition is effectively impossible. The fact that climbing aboard a train in Britain will cost you up to six times what it costs elsewhere in Europe is, it is said, a tribute to the triumph of privatisation. And the fact that Thatcher's flagship policy of selling council houses to their tenants has led, over time, to sky-high property prices and a widespread absence of sensible affordable housing in the places where it's most needed is not proof of the stupidity and short-sightedness of theft from public provision but evidence of bold political daring.

History belongs to the victors. Conservatives in Britain command not just the economy but the narrative as well, and three recent Labour governments have done little to challenge it. *The Blue Touch Paper* aims, among many other things, to make a small contribution towards exposing the idea that everything was chaos until 1979, since when everything has been bliss. The 1970s were disputatious times, times of profound and often bitter argument. Living through them was not easy, and a lot of us, under sustained fire in the performing arts from both right and left, suffered wounds which took years to heal. I'm not sure they have healed. Because they felt so much was at stake, people were ready to argue about plays, about books and even about paintings with the same vehemence with which they argued about how the country should be led. But the political discussions we were having – in particular about how the wishes of working-class employees could be more creatively taken into account – were about important things, things which, disastrously, present-day politicians disdain to address. The shocking rancour of the 1970s now looks like a symptom of their vitality. The flight from subjugation of a mistreated Catholic minority in Northern Ireland looks justified, and the response of Westminster to genuine grievance tone deaf. Today's comparative quiet seems more like a phenomenon of resignation than of contentment.

The premiere of the play *Knuckle*, which brought me to Oxford in 1974, was a youthful pastiche of an American thriller, relocating the myth of the hard-boiled private eye incongruously into the Home Counties. Curly Delafield, a young arms dealer, returns to Guildford in order to try to find his sister Sarah who has disappeared. But, in the process, he finds himself infuriated by the civilised hypocrisy of his father Patrick Delafield, a stockbroker of the old school. In the play father and son represent two contrasting strands in Conservatism. Patrick, the father, is cultured, quiet and responsible. Curly, the son, is aggressive, buccaneering and loud. One of them sees the creation of wealth as a mature duty to be discharged for the benefit of the whole community, with the aim of perpetuating a way of life which has its own distinctive character and tradition. But the other character, based on various criminal or near-criminal racketeers who were beginning to play a more prominent role in British finance in the 1970s, sees such thinking as outdated. Curly's own preference is to make as much money as he can in as many fields as he can and then to get out fast.

The first thing to notice about my play is that it was written in 1973. Margaret Thatcher, you will recall, was not elected until six years later. So, whatever the impact of her arrival at the end of the decade, it would be wrong to say that she herself brought anything very new to a Tory schism which had been latent for years. Surely, she showed power and conviction in advancing the cause of the Curly Delafield version of capitalism – no Good Samaritan could operate, she once argued, unless the Samaritan were filthy rich in the first place – but one thing she certainly was not was John the Baptist. How else to explain the fact that the very split which she confronted between the different mindsets within her government – she named the two opposing sides 'wets' and 'dries' – was explored in my work at the Oxford Playhouse over five years before? In 1951, resolving never to vote for them again, the Oxford novelist Evelyn Waugh had complained that the Conservative Party in his lifetime 'had never put the clock back a single second'. But the administrations which Thatcher first led and then inspired have never shown interest in conserving anything at all. The giveaway, for once, has not been in the name.

You may say that the party aims, like all such parties, to keep the well-off well off. That, never forget, is any right-wing grouping's underlying mission, which will offer a blindingly simple explanation for the larger part of its behaviour. And for obvious reasons the money party in this particular culture has also aimed to sustain the narcotic influence of the monarchy. But with these two exceptions, it's hard to think of any area of public activity – education, justice, defence, health, culture – which any of the last seven Conservative governments have been interested in protecting, let alone conserving. On the contrary, they have preferred a state of revolutionary protest, complaining that, in an extraordinary coincidence, almost every aspect of British life except retail and finance is incompetently organised. Who could have imagined it? And after all those dominant Conservative governments! In this belief, they have launched waves of attacks against teachers, doctors, nurses, police officers, soldiers, social workers, civil servants, local councillors, firefighters, broadcasters and transport workers – all of whom they scorn for the mortal sin of not being bankers or entrepreneurs.

For a party that is meant to like people, and to believe in enabling them, the modern Conservative Party, once inclusive, has had, to say the very least, a funny way of showing it. From every government department we regularly expect sallies against the very people who toil in the sector which the minister is supposed to lead. If there were at this moment a Ministry of Fruit-Picking, you can be damn sure that the only way an ambitious Tory minister could advance his career would be by launching a blistering attack on the feckless indolence and inefficiency of fruit-pickers.

It would be dishonest, however, to pretend any kind of nostalgia for the earlier, smugger form of Conservatism. It is said that leaders like Harold Macmillan – Chancellor, inevitably, of Oxford University – had either fought in the trenches or known men at first hand in their industrial constituencies and so gained a respect for working-class life which the twenty-first-century leadership, with its upmarket aura of fine wine and evenings spent manspreading with sofa-sprawled box sets, conspicuously lacks. But this is to ignore the repellent layer of snobbery on which such sympathy relied.

You may well find the modern snobbery of a Notting Hill Cameron, who would rather be seen to be cool than to be caught out being compassionate, even more disgusting than the old-fashioned kind, because it is so much more cynical and calculated. However, there was in the blimpish tone of the old Conservatism an air of right-to-rule which saw the country as its plaything and government as its entitlement. Winston Churchill's outrage at being booted out at the end of the Second World War and the ruling class's linking of the words 'inexplicable' and 'ingratitude' in the face of the hugely beneficial result speaks of an entire class culture which had at its heart a group resolution neither to understand nor to explain.

In the play *Knuckle*, the author did not take sides. If his heart lay with anyone, it was with the heroine, Sarah's best friend Jenny, who worked in a bar, and who was as unimpressed by father as she was by son. The play, heard equably in Oxford by a small but earnest audience, who seemed to recognise and relish its central encounters, moved to the West End where it was lynched by reviewers outraged at the presence of an anti-capitalist play in the capitalist West End. What the hell was going on? Keep this stuff on the fringe! As one reviewer later had the honesty to admit, 'I was so outraged by *Knuckle* the event that I could not review *Knuckle* the play.'

Even the presence of Edward Fox and Kate Nelligan, giving among the best performances of their lives, could not redeem the evening from its hubristic insolence in trying to shine a light on a confusion which very few people were yet ready to admit, let alone confront. But as the years have passed, the contradictions within Conservatism have seemed to reach some kind of breaking point at which it is very hard to see how its central tenets can continue to make sense. Admittedly, since the severe recession brought about by the banks, Conservative administrations have found favour with the electorate while Labour has languished. At the election a year ago, Conservatives did scrape together votes from almost 24 per cent of the electorate. But such an outcome has done nothing to shake my basic conviction. In its essential thinking, the Tory project is bust.

The origins of its modern incoherence start with Thatcher. Whatever your view of her influence, she was different from her predecessors in her degree of intellectuality. She was interested in ideas. Groomed by Chicago economists, she believed that Britain, robbed of the easy commercial advantages of its imperial reach, could thenceforth prosper only if it became competitive with China, with Japan, with America and with Germany. For this reason, in 1979, a crackpot theory called monetarism was briefly allowed to destroy one-fifth of British industry in a couple of years. The most effective way of curing the disease, it was argued, was by killing the patient.

As soon as this method had been discredited, Conservative minds switched to obsessing on what they really wanted: the promotion and propagation of the so-called free market. If a previous form of patrician Conservatism had been about respectability and social structure, this new form was about replacing all notions of public enterprise with a striving doctrine of individualism.

It is painful, thirty years on, to point out how completely this grafting of foreign ideas onto the British economy has failed. The financial crash of 2008 dispelled once and for all the ingenious theory of the free market. It had always been held by free marketeers that a free financial transaction was in itself educational. The marketplace was where you learnt. If you sold a product cheaply you would suffer long term and modify your future behaviour. But if you bought a product too dear you would also learn. Your mistake would cost you, and in a world of genuine free enterprise, you would know not to do the same thing again. The only thing, ideologues had argued, that could distort a market was the imposition of unnecessary rules and regulations by a third party, which had no vested interest in the outcome of the transaction and which was therefore a meddling force which robbed markets of their magnificent, near-mystical wisdom. These meddling forces were called governments.

The flaw in the theory became apparent as soon as it was proved, once and for all, that irresponsible behaviour in a market did not simply affect the parties involved but could also, thanks to the knock-on effects of modern derivatives, bring whole national economies to their knees. In practice, pollution spread way beyond the parties involved. The crappy practices of the banks did not punish only the guilty. Over and over, they punished the innocent far more cruelly. Ordinary people, who had never even known of these corrupt transactions, let alone understood them, let alone taken part in them, were being thrown out of their homes and put on the street. It was not their stupidity or their greed which was being penalised. They were bystanders, nothing more. Regardless, the supposedly pure transactions of the under-regulated market had spilled over to contaminate their finances and wipe them out.

The myth of the free market had turned out to be exactly that: a myth, a Trotskyite fantasy, not real life.

To everyone's surprise, disciples of Milton Friedman in Chicago were willing to admit the scale of the rout. They used the words 'back to the drawing board'. But in an astonishing act of corporate blackmail, the banks themselves then insisted that they be subsidised by the state. The very same taxpayers they had just defrauded were forced to dig in their pockets to pay for the bankers' crimes. So much, it seemed, for the educational benefits of the free market. Here was a sector which, Lehman Brothers apart, was to be expensively exempted from the rigorous process of learning. Although state aid could no longer be tolerated as a good thing for regular citizens, who, it was said, were prone to becoming depraved, spoilt and junk-food-dependent when offered free money, subsidy could still be offered, when needed, on a dazzling scale, to benefit those who were already among our country's most privileged and who were, by coincidence, the sole progenitors of its economic collapse. What a stroke of luck!

Socialism, too good for the poor, turned out to be just the ticket for the rich.

It was the Labour government of Gordon Brown who consented to this first act of blackmail. It had little choice. There were dark threats from the banks of taking the whole country down with them. But it was the City-friendly Conservatives, learning nothing from history, who caved in without protest to a second, more outrageous wave of blackmail. The banks which had led us into the recession argued that they were the only people who could lead us out. And the only way they could restore prosperity, they insisted, was by returning unpunished to the same practices which had precipitated the crisis in the first place. Just as Afghan farmers believe that only by growing opiate poppies can Afghanistan survive, so Boris Johnson, the Mayor of London and another Balliol boy, insisted that only by French-kissing Canary Wharf and forgiving it everything could Britain get back. Many people have pointed out how mysterious it is that no single individual from the financial world has gone to prison for their offences. But what is stranger still is that those individuals have the brass neck to go on preaching something they call a free market when they themselves have so benefited from a market that has been feloniously rigged in their own favour.

Further, it has become impossible for any Conservative to argue for a free market when they do everything in their power to forbid free movement of labour. One is impossible without the other. A market, by definition, cannot be free if it operates behind artificial walls, or if it excludes traders who can offer their goods and services at a more competitive price. At the moment many such traders are volunteering to arrive and lend our market the very vigour which Conservatives always say it needs. But all too many of them, whether from Aleppo or from Tripoli, are dying with their children in open boats in the Mediterranean because the Home Secretary, Theresa May, who drank the Oxford Kool-Aid at St Hugh's College, is telling them that when she talks of the 'free market', she doesn't mean it. She means 'protected market'. She means 'our market'. She means 'market for people like us'.

How can anyone with a trace of consistency or personal honour stand up and declare that international competitiveness is the sole criterion of national success, while at the same time excluding from that competition anyone who can compete better than you? Economic migrants, showing the qualities of risk-taking, courage, independence and family responsibility which Conservatives affect to admire, are invited by Theresa May to plunge to their deaths in the sea rather than to trade.

The outcome of the Conservatives' thirty-year love affair with the idea that Britain is at heart no different from China, the US or Germany, has inevitably been a sense of threat to the idea of national identity. Once Mrs Thatcher surrendered a native British Conservatism to an American one, she knew full well that the side effect would be to destroy ties and communities that held society together. By her own policies, she was reduced to petulant gestures. At Downing Street receptions, she replaced the despised Perrier with good British Malvern Water, but nobody was fooled. If international capital did indeed rule the world, then nothing made Britain special. On the contrary, it was on its way to being little more than a brand, defined, presumably, by the Union Jack, Cilla Black, Shakespeare, Jimmy Savile, Merrydown Cider, the Bonzo Dog Doo-Dah

Band, and a statesman Thatcher had never met but whom she, assuming unearned intimacy, used to call 'Winston'. 'We are a grandmother,' offered to cameras in the street on the birth of her first grandchild, represented a grammatical formulation halfway between patriotism and lunacy, intended to suggest the unique syntactical glamour of the English language. With the flick of a single pronoun, anyone could make themselves royalty. But on Thatcher's watch, Britishness was just bunting, a Falklands mug, a pretence.

Since Mrs Thatcher, successive Conservative governments have agonised about the problem of how to make citizens loyal to a nation at the very moment when they are declaring the primacy of the economic system over the local culture. Roger Scruton's misty evocations of Englishness have been revered as intimations of a spiritual path from which Tories know they have strayed. Scruton has become the supreme right-wing philosopher of the age not by marking out a path Conservatives have chosen to take, but by adding glamour and mystique to the one they disdained to take. For all their flatulent exhortation, Tory pleas for national cohesiveness have achieved nothing in the way of coherence or impact. Their words die as soon as spoken, because everyone can see that if a government is unwilling to lift a finger to save those few organisations – like, for example, the steel industry – which do indeed forge communities, all their rhetoric is so much guff. Just how many more forgettable videos can there be demanding a loyalty which is not organic and not felt?

The Home Secretary, Theresa May, hitting syllables with a hammer as to a class of backward four-year-olds, glowers as she asks everyone to share what she calls 'British values'. Yet her own values, which she shares with the gilded David Cameron and George Osborne – both graduates of her own Midland madrasa – include support for drone strikes and targeted assassination, the right to intercept private communications, the intention to curtail freedom of speech, the imposition of impossible limits on industrial action, a fierce contempt for any of the sick or unfortunate who have relied on the support of the state in order to stay alive, the creation of a 'hostile environment' for immigrants and a policy of selling lethal weapons to totalitarian allies who use them to bomb schools.

The Home Secretary contemplates with equanimity the figure of the 2,380 disabled people who died in just over two years following Iain Duncan Smith's legislation which recategorised them as 'fit to work'. I don't. By these standards, am I even British? Do I 'share values' with Theresa May? Do I hell? When I hear the Home Secretary demand that British citizens identify with the native culture, I am inclined to remember the words of the novelist James Baldwin: 'Allegiance, after all, has to work two ways; and one can grow weary of an allegiance which is not reciprocal.'

All politics these days is campaigning. None of it is governing. Yes, citizens may indeed owe respect to the party empowered by democracy. But that same party owes respect to the whole country, not just to the tiny bow-tied think-tank faction which inspired their zealotry. When Jean-Paul Sartre was calling for conscripts to refuse service in Algeria, his president, Charles de Gaulle, sent a famous order for him not to be arrested or imprisoned. When asked his reasons, de

Gaulle replied in ringing tones, 'Sartre, c'est aussi la France.' 'Sartre too is France.' What modern British politician is capable of an equivalent generosity?

Once you reduce a country only to its economy, and once you reduce politics to the attempt to prop up the bankrupt and outdated dogma of the free market, your whole practice and frame of reference becomes pinched and morally diminished. Your immune system is down. Who can imagine David Cameron declaring any philosopher, artist or writer whose views he opposes to be 'England too'? When did magnanimity cease to be one of those famous British virtues we are ordered to share?

Margaret Thatcher went out of her way to be as offensive as possible to the people it was her job to represent, declaring that her intention as prime minister was to eradicate socialism once and for all from British life. At the time she said it, 10 million Britons had just voted enthusiastically for a socialist party, led by the patriotic Neil Kinnock. You have only to imagine what the reaction would have been had she said that her aim was to eradicate Catholicism, or Judaism, or football – or gardening. Yet, for some reason, nobody thought it outrageous when she talked about uprooting the most cherished beliefs of well over one-third of the total adult electorate. Why? What new misanthropy gave her the right to declare war on basic notions of the common good, when exactly such notions created the few British institutions which have proved durable and inspiring – the few things which, paradoxically, do give us identity as a nation? The NHS, the BBC, the welfare state.

There will be those of you who think me wistful in imagining that, just because a headbanger's Conservatism no longer makes any intellectual sense, it is therefore finished. You will point, correctly, to the resilience of the Tory Party and its ability to adapt at all times to changing circumstance. In the autumn of 2015, Jeremy Hunt, the Health Secretary, educated at Magdalen College Oxford and therefore well prepared to warn us of what he insisted with relish were the harsh realities of global capitalism – oh God, how Tories love saying 'harsh realities' – insisted that Britain could compete with China only if it lowered state benefits and slashed tax credits for working people. It was, he said, essential for our whole future as a nation. But when George Osborne, the Chancellor of the Exchequer, then reversed his announced plan to slash those tax credits because such slashing would have represented a threat to his own advancement to Downing Street, that same Jeremy Hunt fell, on the instant, obediently silent. Cuts to tax credits, once our only way of beating back the Asian advance, were suddenly perceived as a stumbling block to a fellow Oxonian's career. Whatever their education had taught Osborne and Hunt to believe, it was as nothing to what it had taught them about how to progress.

It is, you may argue, such calculating practicality which is keeping the Tory ship floating long after its engine has died. You will add that the problems of how individual cultures are to endure the assaults of global corporations – which, apart from anything, aim to dodge paying back in tax even a fraction of what they are taking out – are after all not confined to Britain. Even if the government were of a different colour, you may say, even if it had an integrity which Cameron's lacks, it too would be facing the almost impossible challenge of asking how any country is to maintain meaningful democracy in the face of a predatory capitalism run by a kleptocratic class which feels entitled to skim money at will. Would any faction do better than the Tories at dealing with businesses run for no other purpose than their executives' personal enrichment?

Back in 1974, we left Oxford believing we had what is called a nervous hit, and discovered instead in the icy wastes of the Comedy Theatre in Panton Street, just off Leicester Square, that we had something that smelt remarkably like a flop. Because strikes had rendered the heating unreliable, the wind whistled round the legs of the few spectators, while I sat despairing in the pub opposite, drinking Guinness and feeling ill.

Our transfer had not been helped by the announcement of Edward Heath's unexpected election, which had first of all delayed our opening night, and then forced us to premiere unremarked on the very Monday that Harold Wilson's new government was being formed. While we blundered into critical fire, the prime minister was just a mile from our theatre, putting together an administration which he would abandon in a mere two years – perhaps, as we now believe, because he sensed the impending Alzheimer's which would overwhelm him. In the theatre we always have excuses for failure. Few are convincing. Even if we had opened at a more auspicious moment, the play's theme – the toughening of the Conservative venture between one generation and another – would not have been likely to find favour in the merrily commercial theatre of the day.

We ran for four months, mostly to near-empty houses. What saved us? Well, it's an interesting question. Plays in the West End are financed by groups of people, who put money up at the outset, and are later sometimes asked to invest more. In the case of *Knuckle*, a celebrated angel called Edward Sutro, who still turned up to the first night in white silk scarf and carrying white gloves, rang the producer to tell him that he would go on pouring in more money, even though he knew his investment was doomed. He himself was romantically right-wing in his politics, rather like Richard Hillary in whose memory this lecture is given. However, having seen the play, which advanced a view of the world alien to his own, Sutro nevertheless believed, and I quote, that 'without *Knuckle*, the West End would be a much poorer place'.

Such generosity, such de Gaullian breadth of spirit, has a period ring. David Cameron arrived in office aware that a Conservatism which was purely economic could not meet the needs of the country, and therefore choosing to advance an unlikely system of volunteerism which he called the Big Society. It was, self-evidently, a palliative, nothing more, the mere shrug of a faltering conscience, and one which lasted no longer than the life cycle of a mosquito. Alert to a problem, Cameron lacked the fortitude to pursue its solution. Instead, Conservative ministers have fallen back on the more familiar, far more routine strategy of sour rhetoric, petulantly blaming the people for their failure to live up to the promise of their leaders' policies. Do you have to be my age to remember a time when politicians aimed to lead, rather than to lecture? Is anyone old enough to recall a government whose ostensible mission was to serve us, not to improve us?

Commentators excoriate the politics of envy, but the politics of spite gets a free pass. Jeremy Hunt, the Health Secretary, hates doctors. Theresa May, the Home Secretary, despises the police. John Whittingdale, the Minister of Culture, resents public broadcasters. Chris Grayling, once Justice Minister, loathed prison officers and Michael Gove, Minister of Education, had it in for teachers. Nowadays that's what's called politics and that's all politicians, Conservative-style, do. They voice complaints against a stubborn electorate which is never as far-seeing or radical as they are.

Like Blair before him, Cameron has reduced the act of government to a sort of murmuring grudge, a resentment, in which politicians tell the surly people that we lack the necessary virtues for survival in the modern world. They know perfectly well that we hate them, and so their response is to hate us back. Politics has become a sort of institutionalised nagging, in which a rack of pampered professionals, cut from the eye of the ruling class, tells everyone else that they don't 'get it', and that they must 'measure up' and 'change their ways'. Having discharged their analysis, the preachers scoot off through wide-open doors to fortieth-floor boardrooms to make themselves frictionless fortunes as greasers and lobbyists – or, as they prefer to say, 'consultants'.

Of all the privatisations of the last thirty years, none has been more catastrophic than the privatisation of virtue. A doctor recently remarked that she was happy to put up with long hours and underpayment because she knew she was working in the service of an ideal. But, she said, if the NHS were so reorganised that she was asked to work as hard to provide profits for some private health company, she would walk away and refuse. In describing her motivation, she put her finger on everything that has gone wrong in Britain under the tyranny of abstract ideas. Why do we work? Who are we working for? People are ready, happy and willing to do things for our common benefit which, believe it or not, they are reluctant to do if it's all in the interests of companies like British Telecom, Virgin Trains, EDF Energy, TalkTalk, HSBC, Kraft Foods and Barclays, outfits which still, after all these years, have so little interest in balancing out their prosperity in a fair manner between their employees and their shareholders.

The reason we have been governed so badly is because government has been in the hands of those who least believe in it. Politicians have become little more than go-betweens, their principal function to hand over taxpayers' assets, always in car-boot sales and always at way less than market value. No longer having faith in their own competence, politicians have surrendered the state's most basic duties. Even the care and detention of prisoners, and thereby the protection of citizens from basic danger, has been given to contractors, as though the state no longer trusts itself to open a gate, build a wall, or serve a three-course meal.

When cleaners in the Foreign Office work for less than the London Living Wage, our Foreign Secretary, without shame, declares that it is not his problem because he has taken on a private cleaning firm to wash Gilbert Scott's colonial palace. When the same cleaners write a letter to that eminent graduate of – how did I know it would be? – University College Oxford, to draw attention to their exploitation, they are suspended or made redundant. Is it surprising that politicians poll below any other professional group in the country? If abject representatives like Philip Hammond no longer have the human decency to look out on behalf of the people who wipe clean the very floors which Hammond soils with his feet, what are they for? With foreign policy delegated to Washington, and consciences delegated by private contract to logistics companies, no wonder the profession of politics in Britain is having a nervous breakdown of its own making.

In the years after World War Two, under successive administrations of either party, we profited from purposeful initiatives, building the welfare state, the housing stock and the NHS. We voted for leaders who shared a common-sense belief that government was necessary to do good. They entered politics partly because they believed in its essential usefulness. How strange it is, then, this new breed of self-hating politicians who want to make a healthy living in politics, while at the same time insisting that the only function of politics is to get out of the way of private enterprise.

Ever since Ronald Reagan, a disciple of Barry Goldwater, announced that he would campaign on a platform of smaller government, it has been an article of faith on the right to insist that the state must play an ever smaller part in the country's affairs. Our current administration advises everyone else to strip back and face the new demands of austerity. Meanwhile, it employs 68 unelected special advisers to fix Tory policy at taxpayers' expense, while ordering a private jet for the prime minister's personal travel. Whatever the minimised role of government in the so-called free market, there is no reason, it seems, why its practitioners should not celebrate their own irrelevance in conspicuous luxury.

How did we get here? And how do we move on?

Prince Charles, questioning a monk in Kyoto about the road to enlightenment, was asked in reply if he could ever forget that he was a prince. 'Of course not,' Charles replied. 'One's always aware of it. One's always aware one's a prince.' In that case, said the monk, he would never know the road to enlightenment. A similar need to forget our pretensions must newly govern our politics. We do not live in a free market. No such thing as a free market exists. Nor can it. The world is far too complex, far too interconnected. All markets are rigged. The only question that need concern us is: in whose interest? In the light of this question, obsessive Tory spasms about Europe are revealed as a doomed attempt to rerig the market even further in their own favour, so that the same exclusion orders which prevent Syrians, Libyans and Africans from threatening our carefully protected wealth should in future keep out overeager Hungarians, Poles, Bulgarians and Romanians. Far from wishing to free the country to open up to compete in the world, anti-European Union sentiment in Britain is, in Tory hearts, about protecting Britain yet more effectively.

The first task British politics has to address is correcting the terrible harm we have done ourselves by assuming that nothing can be achieved through collective enterprise. It is as much a failure of national imagination as it is of national will. When I woke up on the morning after *Knuckle* opened in London, on 5 March 1974, the stinging impact of the play's rejection forced me finally to admit to myself that I was not just a theatre director who happened to write, but that I was, indeed, going to spend the rest of my life as a professional playwright. Almost everything in my life changed at that moment. In the 1980s and 1990s, my attention turned to the people on the front line who helped bind the wounds of communities shattered by Thatcherism. In *Skylight* and *Racing Demon* and *Murmuring Judges*, I was able to portray teachers and vicars and police and prison officers who, newly politicised, saw their job as to try to tackle the everyday problems caused by a reckless ideology.

I loved writing about such hands-on practical people because I admired them. They became my heroes and heroines. But even as I tried to discredit the publicity which saw Thatcherism as liberating, I was still reluctant to propose a counter-myth which pictured the government of 1945 as a permanent model of perfection. Requested over and again to write films and plays about the National Health Service, I always refused because I was reluctant to make too facile a comparison. How could I write on the subject without seeming to imply that once we had ideals, and that now we didn't? Although I loved the sensual pleasures of writing about the 1940s in *Licking Hitler* and *Plenty*, I was never willing to make the period out to be utopia.

Our current politics are governed by two competing nostalgias, both of them pieties. Conservatives seek to locate all good in Thatcherism and the 1980s, and in the unworkable nonsense of the free market, while Labour seeks to locate it in 1945 and an industrial society which, for better or worse, no longer exists. And yet issues of justice remain, and always will. Conservativism, as presently formulated, is unworkable in the UK because it continues to demand that citizens from so many different backgrounds and cultures identify with a society organised in ways which are outrageously unfair. The bullying rhetorical project of seeking to blame diversity for the crimes of inequity is doomed to fail. You cannot pamper the rich, punish the poor, cut benefits and then say, 'Now feel British!'

There is a bleak fatalism at the heart of Conservatism which has been codified into the lie that the market can only do what the market does, and that we must therefore watch powerless. We have seen the untruth of this in the successful interventions governments have recently made on behalf of the rich. Next, we long for many more such interventions on behalf of everyone else. Often, in the past forty years, I refused to contemplate writing plays which might imply that public idealism was dead. From observing the daily lives of those in public service, I know this not to be true. But we lack two things: new ways of channelling such idealism into practical instruments of policy, and a political class which is not disabled by its philosophy from the job of realising them.

If we talk about British values, the noblest and most common of them all used to be the conviction that, with will and enlightenment, historical change could be managed. We didn't have to be its victims. Its cruelties could be mitigated. Why, then, is the current attitude that we must surrender to it? I had asked this question at the Oxford Playhouse in 1974 as I walked back down a darkened Beaumont Street to a hotel of draped velvet curtains, power outages and guttering candles. I ask it again today.

(2016)

ROWAN WILLIAMS: ESCAPE
FROM SELF

In 2002, when visiting Manhattan, I was surprised to find a photo of Rowan Williams pinned proudly on the fridge of my two best friends. As they remarked at the time, 'Who'd have thought a couple of New York Jews would have a Welsh churchman for a hero?' It was just at the time when Williams was about to be enthroned, and from three thousand miles away they had already noticed that at last we had a public figure in the West who was something other than an easy object of contempt. Better still, once taking up office, he might have some interesting things to say.

It is so deep in the nation's prejudice to believe that the Church of England is weak and wishy-washy that the thoughtfulness and radicalism of this Welsh poet and priest tend to get overlooked. Even when, three weeks ago, he edited the *New Statesman* and made some clear-sighted observations about both the Coalition and the Labour Party ('We are still waiting for a full and robust account of what the left would do differently'), the right-wing press couldn't stir itself to offer much more than a routine lather. Because Williams often speaks in public in a regulation-issue churchy voice, tone can tune out content. But this is a man, remember, who in 1985 was arrested outside the US airbase at Lakenheath. What was his offence? He was singing psalms.

The only time I had met Williams before this interview was for a *Newsnight* discussion during the 2008–9 banking crisis about which the Archbishop had been eloquent: 'Every transaction in the developed economies of the West can be interpreted as an act of aggression against the economic losers in the worldwide game.' Williams came upon me in the make-up room. I was waiting for Jeremy Paxman and passing the time by writing my diary. When he asked me about its contents, I admitted it was the usual unattractive mix of whingeing and self-pity. I said I thought that his own diary, recording his fractious years as Archbishop, would be far more interesting. Did he keep one? He said he didn't, but that he feared, if he had, it would have been pretty much like mine.

Even at the time, I thought this an odd revelation. Like Barack Obama, Williams seemed a good man dealt an impossible hand. If you had happened, at any point, to follow the unending rows about gay clergy and women bishops, it was obvious that the Archbishop had endured a great deal from some insufferable oafs in the higher reaches of Anglicanism who had always been ready to pretend that their lack of Christian kindness towards colleagues was somehow justified by faith. A friend of Williams had even described his period of office as a crucifixion. But even so, I had read enough of his distinctive theology to know how strongly he felt that Christianity should be an escape from self, not an indulgence of it.

'Jesus', he had written, 'is the human event that reverses the flow of human self-absorption.'

For me it was a great privilege to be able to question him properly, this time by strolling down Miss Havisham's draughty corridors all the way to his vast study in Lambeth Palace. It's amazing that such an enormous room can be overwhelmed by files, papers, candles and icons, but it is. If the Archbishop's echoing, cavernous mind sometimes seems to resemble this room, that's because he's both prodigiously learned and, perhaps to the frustration of his admirers in New York, now also considerably more guarded. 'I know some people may find this rather difficult to believe, but I just don't see myself as an individual public commentator. The first thing is to try to hear what's not being said and weave that into the public discourse. Of course, there are occasions when, as a teacher, I do want to say what I think about the ideal social order, but the tar-baby morass of argument about what I think myself is not a place I want to go. After half an hour of wrestling with the tar baby you're immersed in the tar. Things get lost.'

I point out that, in aiming solely to give voice to the voiceless, he sometimes seems reluctant to draw some very obvious conclusions. To me, for instance, a political editorial which asserts that 'we are being committed to radical, long-term policies for which no one voted' is implicitly accusing the Conservative Party of deceit. Surely, we all know Tory politicians went into the election with one agenda, and dishonestly started implementing another? Why doesn't he say so? 'No, I genuinely don't think it was a deceit. In a coalition, policies get pooled. And there was a degree of "We've got to sort this financial question out quickly, and if that means radical cuts, radical restructuring, then we'll do it. Whatever the cost." I wouldn't even call it breach of trust, because again that suggests there's a line of betrayal. I really, really don't think it's that. But I do think the marriage between a localist agenda and a difficult financial squeeze means people don't feel able to see these changes as a vision of the former. They see it as the latter.

'The 1944 Education Act isn't the Law of Moses, but there's something about it which says we need to have a coherent national policy for the delivery of standards. We need to have the kind of system which supports the less advantaged. Now the sense in some of our schools is that things are going a lot more quickly than is comfortable for people to feel confident. You can unravel things, but they will take a long time to put back together.'

The Archbishop is resigned to the inevitability of being misrepresented ('Did you know the editorial would excite the press?' 'I had a shrewd suspicion.' 'Are you now immune to it?' 'Not entirely, but I'm inured to it.'), but on occasions, I suggest, it happens because he lifts the knife, then fails to plunge it in. When he observes that economic relations as they are currently played out threaten people's sense of what life is and what reality means, then surely what he's really saying is that capitalism damages people? To my surprise, he agrees. Does he therefore think economic relations should be ordered in a different way? 'Yes.' So is it fair to say that he's anti free-market capitalism? 'Yes,' he says and then roars with laughter. 'Don't you feel better for my having said it?'

He goes on to rehearse what he insists he's said before ('I don't mind saying it again') about how no one can any longer regard the free market as a naturally beneficent mechanism, and how more sophisticated financial instruments have made it even harder to spot when the market's causing real hurt. But he sounds more passionate when he relates his theories to his recent experiences in Africa. 'I came back yesterday morning from the Congo. What I've been looking at there and in Kenya is localism of a certain kind. The Church is doing really remarkable things with new farming techniques, in a cluster of villages. Things like a biogas project to prevent the cutting down of trees for fuel – very low-investment, very low-technology solutions. I think one of the most moving experiences – yes, moving – was at a village in Kenya which had, thanks to the work of the local church, rethought its farming practices, restocked with indigenous plants, begun to explore very tentatively local fisheries and, out of the modest profits, was just about to start credit-union arrangements for the whole community. Now that's localism, if you like.'

I can't help responding to his enthusiasm by noticing that he seems to be one of those people who always sound refreshed when talking about the micro picture and depressed when contemplating the macro. 'There's a lot in that. Because I'm refreshed by the micro, I have to check myself and ask, "OK, so what's the macro?"' In the Congo, he says, he has been impressed by his meetings with youngsters who've been abducted and brutalised and women who've been raped. He had realised there was nobody but the Church to hang on to these people. 'Especially the youngsters who'd been in the militias. They talked about how the Church hadn't given up on them. Their own communities wouldn't receive them back because of where they'd been and what they'd done. But the Church tried to keep the door open.'

Williams starts to josh me when I say how struck I have been by the depth of his belief in the Church ('Headline: Archbishop believes in Church') but I assure him I am not being facetious. In fact, I've wondered whether the attitude he displays in his writings – 'We can trust the Church because it is the sort of community it is . . . I have seen the Church and it works' – has left him obsessively frightened of schism. Is he paying too high a price for keeping together people who believe different things about gender, priesthood and sexuality? 'I've no sympathy for that view. I don't want to see the Church so Balkanised that we talk only to people we like and agree with. Thirty years ago, little knowing what fate had in store, I wrote an article about the role of a bishop, saying a bishop is a person who has to make each side of a debate audible to the other. The words "irony" and "prescience" come to mind. And, of course, you attract the reproach that you lack the courage of leadership and so on. But to me it's a question of what only the Archbishop of Canterbury can do.'

It's striking that throughout his eight years in charge Williams has been touring as God's fairground boxer, willing to go five rounds with all-comers. Up steps A. C. Grayling, next day Philip Pullman. But his fondness for quoting St Ambrose – 'It does not suit God to save his people by arguments' – suggests how little store he sets by such encounters. 'Oh, look, argument has the role of damage limitation. The number of people who acquire faith by argument is actually rather small. But if people are saying stupid things about the Christian faith, then it helps just to say, "Come on, that won't work."

'There is a miasma of assumptions: first, that you can't have a scientific world view and a religious faith; second, that there is an insoluble problem about God and suffering in the world;

and third, that all Christians are neurotic about sex. But the arguments have been recycled and refought more times than we've had hot dinners, and I do groan in spirit when I pick up another book about why you shouldn't believe in God. Oh dear! Bertrand Russell in 1923! And while I think it's necessary to go on rather wearily putting down markers saying, "No, that's not what Christian theology says" and "No, that argument doesn't make sense", that's the background noise. What changes people is the extraordinary sense that things come together. Is it Eliot or Yeats who talks about a poem coming together with an audible click?' (I later discover it's Yeats: 'A poem comes right with a click like a closing box.') 'You think, yes, the world makes sense looked at like that.'

I ask him if that's the criterion – that the world should make sense. 'Make sense not in a great theoretical system, but that you can see the connections somehow and – I tend to reach for musical analogies here – you can hear the harmonics. You may not have everything tied up in every detail, but there's enough of that harmonic available to think, "OK, I can risk aligning myself with this." Because you're never going to nail it to the floor, and eat your heart out, Richard Dawkins!

'You know that scene in the Woody Allen film where they have an argument in a cinema queue, and Marshall McLuhan is standing behind them and able to interrupt to settle the argument? Woody Allen turns to the camera and says, "Wouldn't it be wonderful if life were like that?" Well, no Marshall McLuhan will ever step forward in the queue and say to Richard Dawkins, "The Archbishop's right." It's not going to happen.'

Williams speaks so gingerly about human beings, always unwilling to impute motive, that it's shocking when you move on to theology and realise how uncompromising his version of God is. He rarely uses the word 'faith'. He prefers the word 'trust', because, he says, 'It sounds less like product placement.' In print, he goes out of his way to emphasise that God doesn't need us. 'We must get to grips with the idea that we don't contribute anything to God, that God would be the same God if we had never been created. God is simply and eternally happy to be God.' I ask him how on earth he can possibly know such a thing. 'My reason for saying that is to push back on what I see as a kind of sentimentality in theology. Our relationship with God is in many ways like an intimate human relationship, but it's also deeply unlike. In no sense do I exist to solve God's problems or to make God feel better.' In other words, I say, you hate the psychiatrist–patient therapy model which so many people adopt when thinking of God? 'Exactly. I know it's counter-intuitive but it's what the classical understanding of God is about. God's act in creating the world is gratuitous, so everything comes to me as a gift. God simply wills that there shall be joy for something other than himself. That is the lifeblood of what I believe.'

I say that's all very well, but how can he be so critical of self-absorption when he himself is a poet? Surely self-study is necessary to create art? 'Ah yes, two very different things. Self-absorption means thinking the most interesting thing in the world is myself. Self-scrutiny, on the other hand, is very deeply part of the Christian experience.' So is his religion a relief, a way of escaping self? 'Yes. We are able to lay down the heavy burden of self-justification. Put it this way, if I'm not absolutely paralysed by the question "Am I right? Am I safe?" then there are more things I can ask of myself. I can afford to be wrong. In my middle twenties, I was an angst-ridden young man, with a lot of worries about whether I was doing enough suffering and whether I was compassionate enough. But the late, great Mother Mary Clare said to me, "You don't have to suffer for the sins of the world, darling. It's been done."'

As we both relish this, my time as his guest is nearly up, but not before I throw out a succession of quick questions, designed to throw him off-balance.

'If you could change one thing about British society what would it be?'

'A more realistic prison policy.'

'If you could change one thing about the Church?'

'Rethink the General Synod.'

'What music will you have at your funeral?'

'Bach and a bit of Dowland.'

'In 2007 you called people who want to attack Iran or Syria as criminal, ignorant and potentially murderous. Do you still feel that?'

'Yes.'

'Libya?'

'Protect civilians, fine, stand up for reconstruction. But look at the experience of the last ten years.'

But even as he screws up his eyes in response to my bullying, I can tell he's longing to return to the subject of poetry and to give me a book of his own.

Earlier in the conversation Williams has attributed to Auden a quotation about poems never being finished, only abandoned.

For the pleasure of forever being able to boast that I've gambled with the Archbishop of Canterbury, I have tried to bet him £5 that it's Eliot. (Research later reveals we're both wrong. It's Valéry. Money to charity, of course.) So, as he signs a dedication, I ask him if he's happy to be thought of in a tradition of Welsh poet-priests – George Herbert, Gerard Manley Hopkins, R. S. Thomas? 'I always get annoyed when people call R. S. Thomas a poet-priest. He's a poet, dammit. And a very good one. The implication is that somehow a poet-priest can get away with things a real poet can't, or a real priest can't. I'm very huffy about that. But I do accept there's something in the pastoral office which does express itself appropriately in poetry. And the curious kind of invitation to the most vulnerable places in people which is part of priesthood does come up somewhere in poetic terms.

'Herbert's very important to me. Herbert's the man. Partly because of the amazing economy. The absolute candour of the poet when he says, "I'm going to let this rip, I'm going to see where this feeling takes me. I'm feeling I can't stand God, I've had more than enough of Him. OK, let it run, get it out there." And then just as the vehicle is careering towards the cliff edge there's a squeal of brakes. "Methought I heard one calling, *Child!* / And I replied *My Lord.*" I love that ending, because it means, "Sorry, yes, OK, I'm not feeling any happier but there's nowhere else to go." Herbert is not sweet.'

'And you like that?'

'Non-sweetness? I do.'

(2011)

WHAT'S A BRITISH FILM?

Nobody is going to thank you for saying so but it's obvious that some of the most outstanding films in British cinema have been made by people who weren't born here. You only have to think of *Repulsion* (Polanski), of *The Servant* (Losey), of *Saturday Night and Sunday Morning* (Reisz), and of *Blow-Up* (Antonioni) to realise that, on occasions, it will only enrich a culture when someone can bring a little anthropological distance to the task of portraying the natives. But even so, it doesn't seem as if anyone who writes about the British film industry has yet remarked on the special weirdness of the calendar year before last. In 2001, four of the gutsiest and most memorable films to be made on these islands were all directed by foreigners.

Honour has rightly been done to Robert Altman, who came from America to make new what many of us had long grown bored with. The rites and rituals of the upper classes were refreshed in front of our eyes in his film *Gosford Park*. And critical justice greeted Paweł Pawlikowski, whose *Last Resort*, an intimate portrait of the random victims of our creaking asylum arrangements, was acclaimed. But how many people took note of Fred Schepisi, the Australian film-maker who went down the same muddy Kent estuary as Pawlikowski to make a mordant and poetic film from Graham Swift's novel *Last Orders*? And why, I wonder, were the British not quite as taken as their European counterparts with the insolence of Patrice Chéreau, who dared to use Hanif Kureishi's story *Intimacy* to make the most thoughtful British film of the year? Home-town audiences seemed outraged that a Frenchman should set out to discover perverse and disturbing beauty in the streets of New Cross.

Evidently, the whole question of what may be said to constitute a British film becomes less clear with time. The collapse of Channel 4's film-making arm has inevitably made cinema-goers nostalgic for the days when that pioneering channel saw its brief as to try further to develop the exhilarating British television tradition of turning a camera onto contemporary life by encouraging work which was always as strong on script as on style. As long as David Rose and his immediate successors were in charge, there was no question of Channel 4 abandoning its admirable commitment to making films about how we live now. It was only when a fresh generation of square-rimmed, crop-haired executives went whoring after Hollywood, crazed by the barren fantasy that the Brits might compete with everything that is uninteresting in American cinema, that Film4 suicided into the sea, making almost as resounding a splash as Goldcrest before it.

It has been fascinating in the weeks following the US release of our new film *The Hours* to discover how hard it is to persuade onlookers that what they are watching is indeed a British production. It is as if everyone is ready to accept the right of Americans to make films about us, but they cannot conceive that mere Brits would have the equal right – or indeed the resources – to make films about them. Of course, in trying to persuade people that *The Hours* is not actually an American film, we start with the initial disadvantage that the names of two of America's greatest actresses – Meryl Streep and Julianne Moore – are on the marquee, alongside that of one of Australia's greatest – Nicole Kidman. But when Stephen Daldry first decided to direct the script I had written from Michael Cunningham's Pulitzer Prize-winning novel, he made only one pre-condition. He insisted that Paramount Pictures make the film here.

Years ago, all American studios had outposts in Europe as a matter of course. One of the pleasures of being a young playwright was to be taken in turn by all seven story editors from all seven studios to expensive restaurants where you would discuss ideas both of you knew would never get made. But those days are long gone. It required Stephen Daldry's exceptional stubbornness to persuade Paramount that it would be worth their while to form a new British company specifically to make this particular film. Thanks to the insistence of the American producer Scott Rudin and the British producer Robert Fox, 95 per cent of the movie was made in the Home Counties. The film had an entirely British crew, a British screenwriter and a British director.

Now that I have given over three years of my life to *The Hours*, to its continual drafting and redrafting, and to helping with its realisation and its dispatch into the world, I can see that in one important aspect only did we make a film which is not typically British. A budget of over $20 million is small by American standards, but over here it is large, and it allows you to lavish a level of thoughtfulness on the actual process of film-making which is not always possible with less money. You buy time – time to make mistakes, and time to go back and correct them. This doesn't, God knows, guarantee that you'll make a better film – on the contrary, you might say, thinking of Stephen Frears, Ken Loach and Alan Clarke, that the sheer speed of a British shoot has often been in direct relation to its excellence – but it does mean you'll make a different kind of film. *The Hours*, I hope, isn't more stately in its execution than most British films, but, for better or worse, there was enough cash to allow it to be deeply considered in its making. Not much has arrived on the screen by accident.

It seems appropriate. Not only is the film's provenance hard to fix, so is its genre. When, as a student, I first became interested in the cinema, it was, in part, through magazines like *Movie* which approached the whole art as one which was grouped into rigid, traditional forms – western, thriller, biopic. Forty years later, when nearly all my friends from my own generation have stopped going, and when my wife and I are often the oldest people in the Odeon, it is striking how bored and bankrupt those genres have become.

It is as if, one century into the new art form, the attentions of the audience can no longer be held by the simple mimicking of our own nostalgia for Hitchcock, for Hawks and for Eisenstein. Although we love our parents, we have to leave home. The three most exciting works I have seen in the past few months – *Dirty Pretty Things*, *Talk to Her*, and the astonishing Finnish film *The Man Without a Past* – all share in common a resolve not to lapse into the exhausted and familiar formulae which make you feel you have seen a film before it's begun.

François Truffaut said that if he walked into a casino, his first instinct would be to master the rules. Godard's first instinct, Truffaut added, would be to invent new ones.

My impulse to get involved in a film of *The Hours* came not just from my ambitions as a screenwriter but also from my frustrations as a cinema-goer. Many people had explained to me that Michael Cunningham's striking novel, a complex, contemporary rewrite of *Mrs Dalloway*, had already been declared unfilmable by every executive who had bothered to read it. But the subtext of their pessimism was something far subtler and more interesting. What they really meant was that no model for how to film *The Hours* could be said to pre-exist. When I realised that Rudin and Fox were inviting me to find cinematic solutions to a story which was set one-third around the act of Virginia Woolf writing a novel in Richmond, England, in 1924, one-third around a woman reading that same novel in Los Angeles in 1950, and the final third around someone in present-day New York whose nickname, to her friends, is also Mrs Dalloway, and who hopes, like her fictional namesake, to give a party that evening, my first reaction was to exclaim, 'Well, that doesn't sound like a film I've seen before.'

It is this timely determination – that we'll make a film that isn't like all the others – which explains the recent popular acceptance of work from Mexico, from China, from Sweden and from Finland in particular. Problems of distribution are still nightmarish. Getting any decent film out of the art-house ghetto remains a soul-destroying undertaking, driven by luck, awards and obsessive self-sacrifice. But powerless national industries do seem suddenly at last at some kind of artistic advantage, placed to meet the exact historic moment at which the Western audience has begun to feel it has seen enough action pictures and dot-com romances to last it a lifetime. 'What did you think of it?' I said to somebody coming out of *The Hours*. 'I don't know,' they said. 'I'll tell you in ten years.'

(2003)

BAD BRITISH WAR FILMS

It was Ralph Richardson's unhappy fate in 1946 to appear in Peter Ustinov's *School for Secrets*, a film which demonstrates nothing except that the invention of radar was a shockingly boring business. But this was by no means the worst war film Richardson ever made. Michael Powell and Emeric Pressburger were wise to forgo credit for their work on *The Silver Fleet*, a 1943 film biography of the Dutch Resistance leader Jaap van Leyden, which says outright what other wartime propaganda had been only implying: 'You all have to die if we're going to win.'

For the post-war audience, cinema-going necessitated over and again revisiting British participation but with all controversy, suffering and complexity removed. It's well known that the David Lean–Noël Coward collaboration, *Brief Encounter*, today regarded as a tremulous classic, was laughed off the screen at its first showing in Rochester. But can anyone believe that Coward commanding a high-camp submarine as Lord Mountbatten – *In Which We Serve* – fared any better? Lean himself recalled serving admirals giggling at the unlikeliness of Coward's performance when they attended the 1942 premiere. My memory throughout the 1950s is of teenage roars of derision at the British splashing around in studio tanks with bootblack on their cheeks to misrepresent their own pasts. Maybe someone was taking this stuff seriously. We certainly weren't.

Immediately after losing office, Winston Churchill restored his fortunes by negotiating what remains to this day the most lucrative non-fiction publishing contract of all time. He received the equivalent of $27.5 million for tilting history just the way he wanted it in his 1,631,000-word book, *The Second World War*. The British film industry was proud to jump to. At a moment when it suited everyone's purposes to pretend the British had won the war alone – the Russians, with their 20 million dead, and the Americans with their superior numbers and materiel barely came into it – no one was happier to turn out on parade than the culture warriors from Rank.

Every self-respecting schoolboy could do mocking imitations of Jack Hawkins in *The Cruel Sea*. 'It's no one's fault, it's the war, it's the whole bloody war,' we would yell delightedly at each other, when faced with any trivial problem. We loved mimicking a legless Kenneth More shouting, 'No sticks for me', before falling flat on his face as Douglas Bader in *Reach for the Sky*. But we looked in something closer to bewilderment at poor Richard Todd getting so upset over the death of his Labrador in *The Dam Busters*. Even in Sussex, in 1955, we knew that anyone, especially Wing Commander Guy Gibson VC, DFO, DSO, who called his pet by the most racist of six-letter words, had grave problems of upbringing.

Our contempt for the cockleshell heroes of British cinema – the film of that name boasts another favourite schoolboy line: 'It may not be the right way but it's my way'; hardly, you might think, what a soldier most wants to hear before battle – did not imply any disrespect or ingratitude towards those who had died. Exactly the opposite. It was because we knew that at least 50 per cent of Bomber Command had never returned that we hated to see their missions travestied into pious melodrama. Growing up, I had already met a bomber who admitted that his own crew were so scared that they dropped their load at the first opportunity, as soon as they had crossed the Channel, regardless of what their proper target was meant to be.

Why did the British cinema never tell us about that?

It's interesting that Second World War films, poor during, got even worse after. As British authority faded in the world, so it was necessary to big ourselves up, to mythologise for reasons more to do with current humiliation than past glory. There were a couple of noble exceptions: Carol Reed and Graham Greene making a masterpiece which told the truth about the black market in post-war Vienna in *The Third Man* (given its world premiere in my own birthplace, Hastings, in 1949) and some members of the SOE banding together during the war to make an authentic amateur film about their work behind the lines, *Now It Can Be Told*.

By 1956, Alain Resnais's account of the concentration camps, *Nuit et brouillard*, had already made most of our native efforts look pretty queasy. If you compare two films about escaping prisoners of war, is there anyone who would claim Guy Hamilton's *The Colditz Story* (1955) has anything like the tension or metaphorical depth of Robert Bresson's *A Man Escaped* (1956)? One is high jinks, the other is a terrifying religious parable. And in 1969 Jean-Pierre Melville blew the British war catalogue off the screen when he made *L'Armée des ombres*. A low-key account of how French Resistance fighters were forced to execute each other in order for the organisation to ensure the security to survive, it is acted by Simone Signoret, Lino Ventura and Paul Meurisse with a deadly, unaffected seriousness which puts our own home-grown fakery to shame.

Today, having learned nothing, some misguided souls want remake *The Dam Busters*. Why? I've seen at least four films about cracking the Enigma code at Bletchley and each one reaches no deeper than the previous. His contemporaries had no idea who Alan Turing was and, having seen all the films, nor do we. We keep scratching away but the reality still eludes us. Remake *The Dam Busters*? And next, will anyone remake *Triumph of the Will*?

(2013)

SAYING GOODBYE TO BLAIR

This was written for the day Blair left office, 27 June 2007. I refer to the 'innumerable' Iraqis who have died since the invasion in 2003. Opinion Research Business had over one million dead by 2007. By 2020, estimates were wildly various, and contested. Some went as high as 2.4 million deaths consequent on the invasion.

New Labour being the project it was, we all have memories of special dismay. My own most lowering moment arrived one night in the winter of 2005 when I went to Chatham House in London to listen to a talk by Gordon Brown, given in memory of the political journalist Hugo Young. I'd only once seen the Chancellor of the Exchequer in the flesh and I accepted the invitation because I wanted to take a citizen's look at our next prime minister. He raced into the room somewhat late, barely acknowledging the friendly audience, and began his speech, which was addressed throughout to the lectern. Repeatedly, in a nervous gesture, he fingered the corners of his apparently unfamiliar typescript, aligning the pages into hospital corners, while motormouthing through its words as though he were a solicitor forced to register a particularly arcane codicil. At the end, he refused questions and swept out of the room at the same pace at which he had entered.

The subject of his speech had been how to restore public trust in politicians. Never once did he use the word 'Iraq'.

Next day in the newspapers I was surprised to see the speech reported as though it were a normal event. Sometimes, you think, the Westminster village is so fascinated with itself that it doesn't even notice when it's being insulted. To an outsider, an infrequent audience at political events, it had been a performance of startling rudeness. But it made its more lasting impression for two quite different reasons. First, it seemed to represent a sort of desolate milestone beyond which no real honesty was any longer possible in the Labour Party about anything. The speech was intellectually derelict. If you had wanted seriously to address the question of why a gulf had grown up between the electorate and the political establishment in Britain, the chances are that you would have been obliged at least to mention, if not to address, the widespread impression that your government had altogether abandoned the notion of an independent foreign policy. You would have had to try to speak to the deep divisions created in the country by a bruising Middle Eastern invasion. But beyond that, I left the meeting saddened because Brown's manner – at once both neurotic and imperious, like a scratchy clip of Charles Laughton as Claudius – contrasted so sharply with my memory of a night ten years earlier when I had gone to another political lecture for the same reason – to get my first proper look at the previous coming man.

The conventional wisdom is to say that Tony Blair 'does' sincerity. Like an advocate, it is claimed, he always believes what he says when he's saying it. But this version of Blair as a gifted snake-oil salesman who happens temporarily to believe in snake oil sells him way short. On that night in the

Queen Elizabeth Conference Centre, the young Blair gave an admittedly routine address, but afterwards in question and answer dazzled everyone present both by his command of subject matter and by the politeness and directness with which he considered everything which was put to him. Again, the common view is to insist that this degree of eloquence and plausibility is suspect, that fluency must be the mark of someone who is up to no good. But anyone whose profession is words is committed to believing that thinking and speaking are often intimately connected. Writers believe that deftness of expression expresses deftness of mind. In Blair's case, at least in 1995, you were left in no doubt that you were listening to the most gifted politician of the period, someone, who, unlike Margaret Thatcher, did not need to resort to childish boasting and bullying to make his points.

All administrations become fractious with age. In their hearts, like most of us, they know the case against themselves better than anyone. Again, like most of us, they live with it daily. Margaret Beckett's impatient advice to Ed Stourton to 'pack it in' when asked about Britain's complicity in countless unnecessary deaths in the Lebanon and Israel last summer served, in her mind at least, as a yet more succinct version of her previous injunction on the same subject to Sky News: 'Oh, for goodness' sake, Adam, leave it alone.' But it also offered the most memorable epitaph to carve on the gravestone of this government: 'Oh, pack it in.' So much has been written, so much speculated in the last twenty years about the contempt the public feels towards politicians, but we hear far less of the reverse – the creeping hatred politicians nurse for us, the stupid and unseeing voters who seem unable to appreciate the complexity and importance of the paramount issues in a dangerous world.

As Victor Hugo said, 'Men hate those to whom they have to lie.'

For, yes, if we are to say along what fault line it was that New Labour was destroyed – be it in Iraq, be it in the NHS, be it in the PFIs, be it in the sardine-packing of the prisons – then surely all its most egregious mistakes flowed from Tony Blair's conviction that he did not need to take any notice of his own natural supporters. He came to believe that he was living his life in some far higher atmosphere, at some more mature level of reality where tough judgements had to be made on the basis of confidential evidence to which only he, the neocons, a couple of dodgy foreign newspaper proprietors and some spies had access. Blair, clearly, had never much liked the Labour Party. He had never thought very highly of those who gave him power. But as time went by, he began to see the popular hostility to his 'higher view' as a mark of authenticity, a sign that he must be facing up to 'difficult' decisions which we, the lazy and the feckless, spend our lives shirking.

It turned out, of course, to be a delusive analysis, most disastrously in the matter of the Middle East, but it was a strangely alluring one. It was also a brilliant answer to those of his critics who had set up a straw man by claiming, quite wrongly, that Blair was nothing more profound than a smooth operator obsessed with popularity. How clever of him, then, to prove the opposite – that he gave not a fig for public opinion! But in detaching himself from the wisdom of the crowd

– the common wisdom, the correct wisdom which could not understand why a mission against Al Qaeda had to be taken into a country where was no trace of Al Qaeda – Blair turned himself into an ungovernable Coriolanus. Here, suddenly, was a man who could not forgive the rest of us for failing to see what he alone sees so clearly. A religious element juiced up the volatile mix of resentment and high stakes. 'If I am persecuted, I must be right.'

This is the paradox: a man who pronounced at the outset that his only ideology would be 'what works' set off on a course which people far stupider, far less gifted than he warned could not possibly work. They were right. He was wrong. Every day we see the lethal evidence of miscalculation, and while mourning for the innumerable victims, for the Iraqis who today say they cannot walk their children to school without passing dead bodies uncollected in the street, we also mourn a man whose tragedy is far deeper than lazy satirists or commentators allow. At a moment when the West needed great secular leadership, it was given instead demented religious leadership. A man who arrived in politics as the voice of modernity and reason became, at his own wish, that most ancient and mystic of figures: the prophet unloved in his own country.

There is, in George W. Bush, his American ally, a shamelessly apocalyptic willingness to admit that judgement on earth means little to him. Bush is happy to tell us he is waiting for judgement in heaven from someone he refers to as his other father. Like many such people with his convictions, he shows few signs of nerves. The decision of the third umpire does not bother him. In Blair, however, there is still, to his credit, a Catholic nervousness, a haunted quality, a knowledge that the road taken was at least a choice. 'I have listened and I have learned,' he announced after a sobering election in 2005, before proceeding wholly to ignore any such lessons in the abject weeks of the Lebanon war.

For us, the spectators, it's been a shocking passage of history. Someone of exceptional strengths became caught up in a situation which brought out every one of his exceptional weaknesses. Because it could happen to any of us, so the facile dismissiveness of his untested critics seems shallow. But at this time of all others, the West needs democrats as its leaders, not martyrs. Pack it in, indeed.

(2007)

LEE MILLER – PERHAPS YOU
HAVEN'T NOTICED

In 2005, Richard Calvocoressi curated a Lee Miller exhibition of portraits at the National Portrait Gallery. I wrote an introduction to the catalogue.

In the spring of the year 2001, the Scottish Museum of Modern Art organised an extraordinary double exhibition. In one of its grey-stone buildings, on one side of a curving Edinburgh road, it displayed the paintings, sculptures and collages of the surrealist critic Roland Penrose alongside some of the best-known items which had once belonged to his private collection, not least Picasso's famous response to the Spanish Civil War, *Weeping Woman*. Just across the way, in even more imposing surroundings, the museum's other, principal gallery offered the most glorious selection yet of the work of the great American photographer who, in 1947, became Roland Penrose's wife. For once, side by side, you could measure the separate achievements of the Collector and the Photographer. But more, you could wonder again at the mysterious circumstances which ensured that the work of one of the last century's most important photographers remained so unknown and so undervalued for so many years. Only since her death from cancer in her husband's arms in June 1977 has Miller's reputation been secured in the way it deserves.

It is hard to imagine an artist from a more singular or disturbing background. Born in Poughkeepsie in 1907, Lee Miller was brought up with her two brothers on a 165-acre farm by parents of Scandinavian descent. Her father Theodore, a keen amateur photographer, saw his hobby as a perfect opportunity to invite the already astonishingly beautiful young Lee and her schoolgirl friends to undress for the camera. They would take up poses which must have seemed, even to what was one of the most progressive families in New York State, openly shocking and lewd. Raped by a family friend at the age of seven, Lee was consequently subjected by her mother – who was also a nurse – to agonising douches of the dichloride of mercury which served in pre-antibiotic days as the primitive cure for venereal disease. By the time, as an adolescent, she had seen a fourteen-year-old suitor fall to his death from a boat in which he was larking around struggling to impress her, Lee had already developed the unusual survival strategies which were to serve her so well – and badly – for the rest of her life.

It is possible, looking at the remarkable book of portraits which Richard Calvocoressi has edited from that Edinburgh exhibition, not only to be dazzled by the exceptional range of a photographer who kept a democratic eye open for young and old, artist and peasant, celebrity and unknown, soldier and civilian alike, but also to see the different phases of what we must take to be Lee's own deliberately segmented life. From the moment in Manhattan when, as a young art student, she stepped out in front of a car to be pulled back onto the kerb by a man who happened, by chance, to be the original owner of *Vogue*, Lee was always determined to change and challenge herself as often as she could. For this twenty-one-year-old, to be discovered by Condé Nast in person and transformed into one of the most successful models in New York was never, in her own eyes, going to get her very far. To this day, she remains one of the few people who may be said to have excelled as much in front of the camera as she did behind. But even as she made her way onto the covers of magazines, and, unknowingly, into the first-ever illustrated ads for sanitary towels – Kotex, as it happens – she was already exhibiting a freedom and generosity in her private life which would put to the test the avowed beliefs and ideals of more than one distinguished European surrealist.

You do not need to be of a mischievous bent to find the story of Lee Miller's arrival in Paris in 1929 intensely satisfying. For years, surrealist artists and film-makers had been proclaiming their belief in a new world in which religion was dead, the family was dead, and life was no longer to be organised into categories determined by office, status or position. In a reimagined universe in which dream and coincidence reigned, and in which apparently random objects belonged curiously together – lobsters with telephones, geese with barrage balloons – it was impossible to retain any outdated notions of personal commitment or possession.

'Love', went the famous surrealist saying, 'is a question of faith.' No one had articulated these beliefs with more passion than the Brooklyn photographer Emmanuel Radnitzky, who had reincarnated himself in Connecticut under the more memorable name of Man Ray. (No question was more guaranteed to infuriate Man Ray than to be asked what his real name was. He had a standby reply for all occasions: 'I am here to inspire, not to inform.') But when Lee Miller walked into the Bateau Ivre, a bar located next to his studio, and asked, unannounced, for a job as his assistant, it was thereafter inevitable that the laddishness of surrealism would be put to flight in the most painful and dramatic way.

Up till then, it had been part of the surrealist manifesto that artists should be able to sleep with whom they chose. Men were free, and women were muses. But when Lee, in her relationship with Man Ray, expected and did not even consider to ask for a corresponding freedom for herself, it was the beginning of the passionate onset of jealousy which would come close to driving Man Ray insane, and which would end in Lee's flight from Paris, back to America and thereafter to Egypt, in order to escape what we would now call Man Ray's stalking.

Chosen by Jean Cocteau to play an armless statue, pursued by an ox, in his film *Le Sang d'un poète*, Miller was, by common consent, one of the most striking women in Paris. A popular champagne glass was moulded from her breast, and her pale hair was cut so short that she looked, in Cecil Beaton's rather regretful words, 'like a sun-kissed goat boy from the Appian way'. It is little wonder that Man Ray, after a tormented two-year relationship in which he was never able to come to terms with Lee's defiant, random sexuality, would react to her eventual departure by losing fifteen pounds in weight in two weeks. More significantly, he became the first in a line of male artists who dealt with their desire for Lee Miller by cutting her image into pieces – in Man Ray's case, by attaching her eye to a metronome and creating the sculpture *Object To Be Destroyed* which carried the written instructions:

Cut out the eye from the photograph of one who has
    been loved but is seen no more
Attach the eye to the pendulum of a metronome and
    regulate the weight to suit the tempo desired
Keep doing to the limit of endurance
With a hammer well aimed try to destroy the whole
    at a single blow

It has become a commonplace of criticism to observe of
Lee Miller's own subsequent career as a photographer, which
lasted until her effective retirement in the 1950s, that it was
her original grounding in the philosophy of surrealism in
Paris which trained her to watch out for the humour and
the sudden juxtapositions which are said to mark some of
her most celebrated images. Calvocoressi, for instance, in
his introduction to his book, draws attention to her faultless
gifts of composition and refers to her flair for 'the telling but
overlooked detail, odd pairings or combinations of unrelated
objects, and dramatic or quirky viewpoints'. And there is no
question that for the rest of her life Miller herself acknowledged
the solid, practical darkroom training of Man Ray, even when,
as in the case of the technique of solarisation, there had been
some dispute as to which one of them had discovered it. But
if we want to identify the particular quality which makes her
work so outstanding, surely it is just as important to insist that
Lee Miller is someone who found her identity as an artist in the
experience of her own adversity, in the habitude of being the
cause of hysteria in others, while being accustomed, essentially,
to remaining calm inside herself.

There is something cool, something level, and something which is, at bottom, unforced in the way the photographer and her camera look at the world. Yes, sometimes Lee Miller shoots a person or an object from an unexpected angle, but even from that angle, there is, in the best of her work, an absence of melodrama, an unheated sense of the inherent beauty and the transitoriness of life, which is uncontaminated by any wish to soup up the images or to use them to make points. 'It's like this,' says Lee Miller. 'Perhaps you haven't noticed. This is how it is.' It is as if, at the heart of the familiar conviction that life may finally amount to nothing but chaos and dream, Lee Miller is that rare surrealist artist who is also able to find, amid that chaos, a simple human dignity and poise. The portraits are not pure portraits. They are placed. Around the face itself, the air is charged, the theatrical props are weighted with a sense of the subject's own deepest history, and an eerie intuitive sense of how the person came to be who they are.

It is clear that if Lee Miller did indeed start out as that special type of photographer who is able to look and to experience, and yet at the same time, in some other part of her being, to hold herself back, it would be only a matter of time before she would find her greatest subject. That subject, more than likely, was going to be war. In the summer of 1939, Lee left Cairo, where she had made what seemed on the surface like a marriage of comfort to an Egyptian businessman, this time in the company of an English art critic and collector with whom she had lately begun an affair. Roland Penrose was a moneyed Quaker, seven years older than Lee, who was one of the few of his fellow countrymen either to understand, or to be excited by, the latest developments in art on the Continent. A painter and collagist himself, he was never able to overcome a testy inferiority complex which was aggravated by his close friendships with Picasso and Max Ernst. When it became certain that war with Hitler was imminent, Roland and Lee drove back across France to set up home together in a terraced Georgian house in Hampstead, she, for her part, determined at the first opportunity to get as close to the action as she possibly could.

For Lee Miller what followed was almost five years of frustration. While Roland, a pacifist and too old to fight, was more than content to join the Home Guard, using his artistic talent to become 'a senior lecturer in camouflage', Lee bullied her way into a job at English *Vogue*, doing what she regarded as a mere stopgap endeavour which would serve to pass the time only until the moment when she was able to go to war. But the policy of the British army that no female photographer would be given accreditation to go into the field left Lee Miller performing tasks which she felt were humiliating and irrelevant. Faster lenses and higher film speeds meant that she was able to take fashion models out of studios and to place them in London's bombed-out buildings and war-damaged streets, creating images which would once have been called surrealist, but which were now seen to be effortlessly everyday. But, finally, whatever the quality of the work – and between 1939 and 1944 Lee Miller did take some of her most accomplished photographs, in particular for the Blitz book *Grim Glory* which was published in 1940 – she nevertheless felt herself wasted and underused, trapped in the thankless business of memorialising frocks and handbags at the very moment when, elsewhere, Europe was tearing itself apart.

You cannot understand Lee Miller's deep feminist need to get herself to the very centre of events unless you also understand her other, equally deep conviction that those events could not damage her. Nothing in the story of Lee Miller is more striking than her own inbuilt certainty that whatever life threw at her, she was, in some way, protected. Rightly or wrongly, she believed herself foredestined to survive. In 1941 she had met the *Life* photographer Dave Scherman, and introduced him into her household with Roland, ostensibly as the Downshire Hill lodger, but more importantly as the third member of a cheerily consensual *ménage à trois*. They all remained friends for the rest of their lives. Lee was drawn to the twenty-five-year-old Dave not for his looks – he was short, dynamic and bespectacled: a contrast to the tall, patrician Roland – nor even for his perfect willingness to take his place as one among three. More important, she was fascinated by him because, as someone who had already escaped from almost two years as a prisoner of the Germans, Scherman was the very embodiment of the modest, happy-go-lucky, seen-it-all wartime professional she most aspired to become.

It was, inevitably, Dave who pointed out to his friend and lover that she had no need to spend her life fighting the sexism of the British Army. *Life*'s Margaret Bourke-White had already made a well-deserved reputation with her photographs from the Russian front, and Bourke-White, like Miller, was American. It was simple. If the reactionary British wouldn't take Lee, the progressive Americans would. One month after

D-Day, Lee Miller found herself landing on a Normandy beach. Choosing to misunderstand the strategic state of play, she made her way on foot into the port of Saint-Malo, which the Eighth Army had not yet successfully secured and, from the centre of the battle – what she later called 'a war of my own' – she took startling images of its bombing and surrender. Within a few days of arriving on French soil, she had not just countermanded military orders and scooped the world press. She had also embarked on a second career. Lee Miller was no longer a humble snapper. She persuaded her editor, Audrey Withers, to let her double in the unlikely role of *Vogue*'s war correspondent.

It is bewildering, looking at the technicoloured pageant of fashion, fake and fame which now guides editorial choices in so many women's monthly magazines, to remember that it was indeed British *Vogue* which once published tens of thousands of words of Lee Miller's graphic war journalism. To their lasting credit, *Vogue* also published her photographs of the inmates of Dachau and of Buchenwald, which she sent back to London, heralded by the unforgettable words in her cable: 'I IMPLORE YOU TO BELIEVE THIS IS TRUE.'

For the nine months between the Allied landing and the long-delayed Allied victory, Lee Miller was everywhere she needed to be, often rash, always fearless, with Rolleiflex and typewriter, out among the American GIs whom she idolised and adored, covering first the liberation of Paris, then the fierce winter campaign in Alsace. Her nose for a story became a joke among her colleagues: 'As soon as Stinky Miller turns up, something's bound to happen.' But even as she worked, always centring herself at the correspondents' favourite Hôtel Scribe in Paris, where she maintained Room 412 in conditions of indescribable untidiness – joined by a connecting door to Dave's 410 – her mood was becoming darker and darker, her behaviour with drink and with men more impossible. Her pictures, interestingly, moved closer and closer to their subjects, as if she were testing the limits of the objectivity she had hitherto found inside her own calm. The war was both feeding her and driving her mad. By the time she sat, like the great model she once had been, naked in Hitler's bath in his abandoned apartment in Munich for Dave Scherman's most famous photograph (she took a matching photograph of Dave, but you don't see that one so often) it was as if she were already gripped by the second of her governing premonitions.

It is, we may say, one of the most terrible of all human truths that the qualities which lead a person to prosper in war do not always serve them so well when peace returns. The day after she had photographed the burning of Hitler's personal mountain hideout at Berchtesgaden, Miller was working on a story when someone brought her news of the German surrender. 'Shit!' she replied, without looking up. 'That's blown my first paragraph.' It was her only response. Lee Miller knew. When the war stopped, so would her life.

For over a year after the ceasefire, in spite of Roland Penrose's desperate pleadings, she refused to return home, 'encased', in her words, 'in a wall of hate and disgust'. Lee was enraged to the point of obsession with the inevitable shabby compromises of the immediate post-war dispensations, and she thereby developed a pathological hatred of everything German which would last her to the end of her life. They had lost. They had killed the Jews. They should suffer for it. They were not suffering enough. 'A more disorganised dissolute dishonest population has never existed in the history books . . . I deplore every ounce of relief sent to the enemy Balkans (that includes Austria) and the perpetrators of the *Daily Mail* campaign should be shot tomorrow's dawn.' Lee Miller took random assignments in Hungary, in Austria – one day, the execution of a fascist prime minister in a Budapest courtyard; another, dying skeletal children in drug-starved Viennese hospitals – all in the hope of being able to believe that there might still be a brief, there might still be a purpose. The regime of Benzedrine, alcohol and coffee took its toll. 'I'm as popular as a leper and as logical as a scattered jigsaw puzzle . . . I'm as happy in my work as a squirrel running in a cage.'

It was only when Dave Scherman, in 1946, by now himself safely re-established in New York, sent Lee Miller a two-word cable 'GO HOME', that Lee was forced to accept that the subject had indeed said a final farewell to the artist. Lee let a week go by and cabled back one word: 'OK.' Her return to England and to a grateful Roland Penrose resulted in pregnancy and the birth of her only child Antony. Lee Miller worked on for *Vogue* for a few more years, without enthusiasm, unable to find the pleasure she once had in pointing a camera, then retired to a farm in Sussex where, terrified of becoming what she and Dave used to call 'foxhole bores' she refused even to mention the work which had once consumed her. When, in the months after her death, the thirty-year-old Antony Penrose went up into the attic to discover the neglected store of 40,000 negatives and 500 prints which would form the posthumous basis of the Lee Miller Archive, it was the beginning of an extraordinary act of filial revelation of a mother who had been largely forgotten – and, to some degree, at her own wish.

There are a hundred reasons for Lee Miller's post-war eclipse, not least the bitterness and alcoholic despair that made her such a difficult companion in later years. But in asking the question of why she was written out of her own profession, it is impossible not to feel that the attitude of the man she had loved played some significant part. As Lee declined into aimless rural rage, seeing life only from the bottom of a whisky glass or over the flyleaf of a recipe book, Roland, by contrast, prospered, founding the Institute of Contemporary Arts and writing a much acclaimed biography of Picasso. 'It is as if I had written it with you,' said Picasso. As the once subversive critic grew, over the years, into an achingly blimpish establishment figure – his autobiography *Scrap Book* contains some unlikely remarks on the Queen's rare and much underestimated feeling for modern art – so Lee sank into a sullenness which was a trial to everyone she knew. 'You bore me,' she would say to everyone. 'You're so boring.' To her son: 'You're a moron.' As Roland swanned around Europe celebrating his friendships with the greatest artists of the day – Braque, Miró, Brâncuşi, Giacometti, Magritte, Chillida and Henry Moore – this leading connoisseur failed to notice – or did he just fail to point out? – that in his bed (and by now in his bed alone) lay another, who, in her own field, has claims to be as great as they.

The final act of masculine revenge: a man looks everywhere for great art except on the pillow beside him.

No one can pretend that Lee's story is anything but overwhelmingly sad. Her independent vitality and adventurousness turned in on itself. At the end, a clear voice chose nothing but silence. Lee set off into life, maybe damaged, maybe not, by the trauma of her early experiences, with unconventional attitudes which served her brilliantly for forty years, but which failed her for the last thirty. Behind her she leaves a legacy that, for some of us, is second to none. Today, when the mark of a successful iconographer is to offer, like Helmut Newton, craven worship of wealth, or, like Annie Leibovitz, a yet more craven worship of power and celebrity, it is hard to imagine an artist of Lee's subtlety and humanity commanding the resources of a mass-market magazine. Photography is now used by editors to seal off the rich and famous, to deny us access, not to grant it. But this young art form was, for a period in the middle of the last century, the means by which the world looked new and strange. The men in the surrealist movement talked their philosophy, but a woman lived it.

(2013)

THE DIVER, LOUIS MALLE

I was just twenty-four when I boarded a late train from Amsterdam in order to see the dress rehearsal of my first play, *Slag*, due its French premiere next day in a glamorous boulevard theatre in Paris. This being France, the three actresses were too busy eating their dinner at ten o'clock at night for the run-through to have even begun. Round about midnight, I looked round the empty stalls, and there sitting waiting patiently for the curtain to rise were, unmistakably, Louis Malle and Costa-Gavras. When I asked what they were doing, they said that they'd heard that the play was going to be interesting, so they'd just turned up. I was able to confide that I was the author.

I'm understating if I say that for me this moment was like a free pass to paradise. Only a couple of years before, I'd left university where I'd ended up running the Film Society. I'd walked out of the Arts Cinema, Cambridge, long past midnight, shaken to the core by Maurice Ronet's determination to kill himself in Malle's *Le Feu follet*. I'd never seen any sequence which compared with Ronet sitting in a café in black and white, doing no more than watching passers-by. Yes, you could read philosophers, you could read tracts, you could, if you wanted, even bother with novels and plays. But much the most stimulating thing to do was to go to your nearest art cinema and see the films of Jean-Luc Godard, of Ingmar

Bergman, of Federico Fellini, of François Truffaut and of Louis Malle. In the 1960s, cinema had become the leading edge of European thought.

I'd barely seen Louis again in the subsequent twenty years before he rang me out of the blue in London in the spring of 1991 and asked me what I was doing. I told him I'd just finished my first attempt at a particularly trying play called *Murmuring Judges*, a critique of the British legal and penal system. Next day, to shake off my gloom, I was planning to jump in a car to go and lie on a May beach in St Tropez. The thing I needed more than anything else in the world, after a sustained period of writerly frustration, was to be alone. Louis suggested I take a book down with me. It was called *Damage*. It was by an unknown writer called Josephine Hart.

The place I always stayed was called the Ferme d'Augustin, a stone's throw from the beach at Ramatuelle, and in those days very much a *hôtel de charme* rather than a *hôtel de luxe*. I liked its simplicity and I liked being alone. Within twenty-four hours of my toes touching sand, Louis rang again, this time from Paris, and asked if he might come down and join me. He had, after all, a long history with St Tropez. I said that his presence would confound my plans and ruin my holiday. He said he'd see me the next day.

Clearly, I knew straight away what he was after. Louis had shown Josephine's novel, about a British politician destroyed by an unaccountable sexual passion, to his old collaborator, the great Jean-Claude Carrière, but Carrière had taken four days to hand-write a complete script – in French, of course – before declaring the work unfilmable. The owner of the *ferme* confirmed that she would indeed have a spare room for a friend of mine arriving tomorrow, but when given the friend's name – Malle – she immediately recalibrated her manner, gearing up into a hitherto concealed mode of attentiveness and high excitement. If she could have swung a jackhammer and knocked through a few ancient stone walls to make a bigger room, she would have done so, on the spot.

Louis was laconic on his arrival, handsome and humorous, the understated star in suede and soft brown fabrics, unsurprised by the flurry of farmgirls who seemed to appear from nowhere to help carry his bags. He wanted to know at once if I had liked the book. I said, very much. Why? Well, I said, I felt that its high poetic style and pure strength of feeling threw a sort of Celtic axe through the plate-glass respectability of the British novel. Louis asked whether this meant I would like to write a screenplay from it. I said I most certainly would not. I was tied up on an intractable theatre piece, and furthermore my recent clumsy experiences in cinema had left me out of love with the medium.

'You're right,' he said. 'Maybe it's foolish to try.'

We spent the rest of the day getting to know each other, though without Louis ever taking off a single layer of his expensive clothing. Like a vampire, he never sat anywhere where the sun might touch him. In the evening, we enjoyed a good sea bass which he explained should always be eaten with red wine – 'In fact, never drink white wine, it will kill you' – and then he suggested that we sit down the next morning at breakfast, and that, purely as an exercise and to help him clear his mind, I should recount the story of the book. I said,

OK, but there was no question of my actually writing the film. He agreed.

This, then, became the pattern of our next ten days. Each morning, in the light spring air, while he sipped his coffee and I ate my croissant – 'Never eat croissants, they will kill you' – I would start out like some nomadic bard or oral poet. Every time I would begin in the same way – 'There's this Conservative Member of Parliament' – and yet barely would I have got to the end of my first sentence before the questioning started.

'Conservative, yes. Now explain to me, what exactly is a Conservative?'

'He meets this woman.'

'Yes. Where? How? What's she wearing? When you say he meets her, what does that mean? Would it be truer to say that she meets him?'

Thus it was we proceeded, using what I came to know as the interrogative method. Progress was slow. I had imagined, exhausted after this first session of extravagant torture, that I would at least be allowed to pick up next day from where I had left off – a mere six pages into the story. 'Now where was I?' I said hopefully on the second morning, before Louis immediately countered with 'No, no, no, let's go back to the beginning.' I could scarcely believe it. Nor could I believe it on each of the successive nine days when, yes, we set off once more from the same dreaded words: 'There's this Conservative Member of Parliament.'

Occasionally, he would allow me off in the late afternoon to enjoy the last rays, while he read something heavy in the shade. In the evening, we would saunter again to a beachside restaurant. Sometimes he would suggest that we call in on Brigitte Bardot, who lived just up the road. But because he had detected my eagerness, and was amused by it, he took pleasure in dangling the prospect, then at once withdrawing it. 'Oh no, let's not see Brigitte, it'll distract us. And the people around her are boring.'

However, after three or four days, even I had to admit that I was becoming like an Olympic athlete, whose punishing hours of training were bringing unnoticed rewards. Much to my surprise, my muscles were starting to ripple. I could even get through whole sentences without interruption. It was as if Louis and I were laying down planks over marshy ground, and together finding a path. Slowly we constructed a watertight narrative, which was secured by the oddest of means: endless repetition. The more often I told the story out loud, the more natural its logic and development seemed to become.

At the end of the ten days, I was able, without notes, to recount the entire story in around twenty minutes. My listener did nothing more than light and relight his pipe throughout. When, for the final time, I got to the dramatic end, our hero disgraced and in lifelong exile, Louis beamed with pleasure and said, 'Well, you might as well write it now. After all, you've done all the work. The script itself will be a formality.'

So saying, he ordered a taxi and disappeared on the next train to Paris.

As it happened, through no fault of our own (I would say), the making of the film was never to be as idyllic as its conception. If the writing was yin, the shooting was yang. Juliette Binoche arrived, an untypical French actor, modest about her great talent and uncertain of her character, while a leather-clad Jeremy Irons rode in on his motorbike, less modest and convinced from his recent Oscar-winning experiences that his own hand was necessary to fashion any screenplay he was required to speak. The off-screen chemistry between them was non-existent. Asked to climb up a sheer cliff of blind trust and desire, the two of them took one look at each other and panicked.

When the film came out, its quality was much disputed. Lots of people seemed discomfited by the theme of the successful man who gives up everything for passion. When I said to the PR representative that I had heard from the producers that the first screening had gone well, she looked at me amazed and replied, 'Who on earth told you that?' Miranda Richardson was acclaimed for an astonishing performance as the wronged wife, but although the role took her to the Oscars, I was never sure whether she cared for the film either. For many years afterwards, I was left in the peculiar position of being the only principal participant who liked the film. I thought Binoche and Irons great. Today when I visit a warm country, Italy, say, or Spain, or when I visit South America, I am hailed with embarrassing fervour as the man who wrote *Damage*. If the subject comes up anywhere more northerly, in chillier places like the UK or on the Eastern Seaboard of the United States, I'm likely to be more coldly appraised.

Louis and I planned more films together. The first time we met after the release of *Damage*, neither of us mentioned it because it had once been a perfect film in our heads, and now it was just something in the cinemas. Instead we discussed why nobody had ever tackled the overlooked first two hundred pages of *Robinson Crusoe*, during which Crusoe is not on an island. But Louis died at Thanksgiving in 1995 before either of us had time to think Defoe's opening through. He was buried after a heart-rending service at Saint-Sulpice in Paris. He was sixty-three. Late last year, after staying firm friends with all conflicting parties, Josephine died too, her own memorial held in Poets' Corner in Westminster Abbey.

Everyone who has ever worked in cinema knows what Eisenstein meant when he said you must go where the film leads you. Louis abhorred the slowness of *Damage*'s British crew because he wanted to work in as fleet a way as he had when he was young with Jeanne Moreau, with Maurice Ronet and with Michel Piccoli. Louis was never part of the French film establishment. Because he was the son of a rich bourgeois family, he was distrusted by some of the less generous members of the *nouvelle vague*. He had a love/hate relationship with France for the rest of his life, although nearly all his films made their money back in France alone. The rest of the world was jam. His friend Mike Nichols liked to debunk the idea of gifted directors like Orson Welles being frustrated by the Hollywood system as 'self-indulgent horseshit'. In Nichols's experience studio heads were 'idiots'. Overbearing executives were always an unconvincing excuse for making a bad film, or not making films at all, because 'anyone with a modicum of savvy can get the better of them'. Louis knew he was lucky because he rarely had to try. His ability to devise films which made economic sense in Europe gave him freedom.

He had spent a whole year going down underwater in a bathyscaphe with Jacques-Yves Cousteau, who said Louis was the best cameraman he ever had. That's why he was so well read. At that depth, you can film for only a few hours. Louis had spent the rest of his day with a book. John Guare, the American playwright, said that Louis had started as a diver, and remained a diver for the rest of his life. His fabulous output – documentary and fiction – was notable for its variety. He made *Lift to the Scaffold*, *The Lovers*, *Le Souffle au cœur*, *Le Feu follet*, *Lacombe, Lucien*, *Au revoir les enfants*, *Phantom India*, *Atlantic City*, *God's Country* and *My Dinner with Andre*. Very few people have ever directed so many good films. (He also made *Black Moon* and *Pretty Baby*. Even the greatest film-makers are uneven.)

Louis taught me the most valuable film lesson of all, the only one worth learning. The more painstakingly you prepare, the freer you will be on the day. All Louis's power, all his extraordinary openness of spirit, came from the fact that he believed the real work on *Damage* had been done, my will bending to his, on a French beach months previously. I never go back to St Tropez.

(2012)

THE YEAR OF MAGICAL THINKING

It sounds odd maybe, callous even, to say that the eighteen months I spent preparing and directing *The Year of Magical Thinking* were professionally among the happiest of my life. When I was first approached by the American producer Scott Rudin in November 2005 to direct a play Joan Didion wanted to write based on her hugely successful book, a couple of friends looked at me sideways. Was I sure? Did I really want to let myself in for such a long time addressing such forbidding subject matter? It was easy enough to spend a few hours reading a book about death which you could let flop in one hand while nursing a drink in the other. But how would it be to spend months in the gruelling Broadway system – endless previews, needless hysteria, erratic critics – in the company of a seventy-two-year-old first-time playwright whose agony of grief was so raw? Wasn't the prospect . . . well, rather austere? So it's hard to explain why my own reaction – the one you have before you can think – was that the whole thing sounded, in prospect, highly enjoyable. I responded to Scott's offer in a loose paraphrase of *Citizen Kane*: 'Great. It sounds like we could have some fun.'

That our time with *Magical Thinking* in New York did indeed reward the whole company and crew with so much pleasure and humour is principally down to the spirit of the author. I had never met Joan before we started to consider how she might imagine a possible play. Nor, when I was first approached, had I even read her latest book. In Britain *Magical Thinking* had not had anything like the impact it achieved in the US: it had not become the indispensable modern handbook to bereavement. At the turn of the century, however, I had written Joan a heartfelt fan letter, out of the blue, one author to another, about her collection of essays *Political Fictions*. She had answered with what I would now recognise as a characteristically courteous and thoughtful reply. It was self-evident to the most casual reader that by keeping herself away from any contact with Washington, Joan was able to define the characters and intentions of the leading imperial figures with far more insight than any Beltway insider. Her methods were deep research, intuition and watching television. But beyond admiring her wonderfully obvious authorial stance – 'Let's talk about politics like we're human beings' – I was struck by how she also made political reporting so fresh, so immediate, by not bothering with piety. Having started out as a roguish if complicated admirer of the ideals of Barry Goldwater, Joan brought to her view of the latest fearful idiots in the White House a marked personal prejudice in favour of courage, order and liberty.

There is, of course, in all Joan's reporting an exciting tension between what appears to be the cool poise of her much admired prose style and the banked-down, vivid heat of her feeling. Subjective and objective are at glorious war. So when I did finally meet her in Scott's offices on 45th Street on a freezing January day in 2006, it was a difficult first step for me to point out to this apparently frail, painfully thin woman

('Under 75 pounds,' she said, 'and you begin to feel the cold') that we were facing an egregious artistic problem.

Since she had written her best-seller about the death of her husband, the screenwriter and novelist John Gregory Dunne, her daughter Quintana had also died, at the age of thirty-nine, after a series of terrifying medical incidents. For that reason, it was impossible to dramatise the book as it was. A mere recitation was anyway out of the question. Joan had written prose. Now we needed a play. But, more damagingly, the character on stage would look unintentionally stupid if she appeared to know less than the audience. How could she alone not know that her own daughter had died? What was required, therefore, was a full-scale reinvention, not only of the events themselves, but of the voice in which the events were recounted. An author who had dug as deep as she could into the madness which overwhelmed her upon her husband's death was being asked by a director she didn't know to subject her feelings for her daughter to a similar pitiless scrutiny.

Nothing is more testing for any writer, however distinguished, than to recast familiar material in a new form. If a work is any good at all, the author will have arrived at a tone, a shape and a progress which all seem right and inevitable. But in asking Joan to start again, and in particular to address the question of who the narrator truly was – for on the clarity of that question depends the destiny of all one-person shows – I underestimated her Hollywood nous. Joan turned out to be an intoxicating mix of artist and hack, the kind of writer whose profound certainty about what they want to say paradoxically makes them completely open to the idea of being edited. In the coming months I would get used to the questions 'How's this?', 'What do you think?' and 'Is this OK?'

One of Joan's special advantages over some of her colleagues was that she and John, as a team, had always been ready to turn their hand, Nick and Nora-style, to what they called 'crash rewrites'. Neither of them had a trace of the unearned condescension with which novelists, in particular, so often fail in the cinema. For them, the collaborative arts were enlivening. Their years spent living on the shore in Malibu had left them both with a realistic, romantic respect for the mad variety of people who work in the movies, and a salty appetite for the industry's gossip. Although Joan had no idea, she said, of how to write a stage play – she had never tried – she was willing to learn on the job. Her first phone call to me after our meeting was practical. Could I do a word count of my own play about Israel and Palestine, *Via Dolorosa*, so she could know how long a theatrical monologue needed to be?

It's important to make clear that *The Year of Magical Thinking* is Joan's. Although I did help frame its architecture, the basic conceit of the evening and every single word of its text belong to one person. From the very beginning Joan had wanted to present the audience with an unreliable narrator, with someone whose response to an unacceptable event had been to find herself unable to accept that it had happened at all. Admittedly, in the months of our work together, I would come to enjoy Joan's mordant sense of humour about her own over-controlling tendencies – her desire to arrange the world just as she wants it and to make sure everyone else in her orbit also sees it her way. But I was well aware of the cost she had paid for being, if you like, the wrong kind of person to experience two sudden bereavements. Just to look at her swathed in scarves and North Face goose feather against the cold was to be reminded that this was a woman who had suffered immoderately.

Joan's first instinct after John's fatal heart attack in their apartment had been to try to 'master' the event by doing everything she could to understand it. If she could marshal the facts, surely she would be able to explain them? Yet the event itself – its finality, its meaning – had continued to escape her. Indeed, the very fact that he was dead had refused to sink in. She had gone on for months thinking him alive. Both she and I relished, therefore, the idea of spending an evening with an unnamed character (Why call her Joan? Why call her anything?) who would begin by reassuring you how well she was coping. As the action progressed, an alarming disparity would grow up between how the character claimed to be feeling and how, in contrast, she came across. Slowly, the audience would come to see that she was indeed mad, heading without realising it for those terrible days in what Joan called 'the vortex': driving round Los Angeles, dressed in scrubs, trying to administer her daughter's serious illness and avoiding any place, sight or person which might trigger memories of her former life.

You may say the story of *The Year of Magical Thinking* is of a woman who has to do what is, for her, the hardest thing in life: to admit her own helplessness. The distinctive power of the play comes from the fact that it is written by a non-believer. Unlike previous popular works on the subject, like C. S. Lewis's equally acclaimed *A Grief Observed*, it offers no comfort. In facing death, Joan tells us we are facing meaninglessness. And yet in spite of the classical seriousness of the theme and the disturbing closeness of the events – Quintana had died at New York Cornell only six months before we began working – I made a conscious decision to behave as if this were a play like any other. Nothing, I thought, could be worse than to go into this project aiming to wrap the author in cotton wool. If she could face down the horror, so could we. Indeed, I suspected the very reason Joan was doing the play was to return herself to a version of normality. The most unhelpful thing I could do would be to go round with a long face.

Later, deep in rehearsals, Joan would recount her anger at a mourner who had come up to her at John's funeral and told her how terrible she must be feeling. Joan had taken the woman's words not as an act of consideration, but of aggression. If she hadn't been feeling terrible before, she certainly was now. But even before hearing that story, I had already decided that I was going to feel free to ask anything I liked. I would aim to create as carefree an atmosphere as I could. Twice, I believe, I accidentally reduced Joan to tears by some particular line of enquiry, both times, I think, to do with Quintana, when, as a mother, she seemed to fall down an unseen, precipitous chasm of memory. But in spite of my occasional clumsiness, I still believe, rightly or wrongly, that Joan shared my conviction that a certain robustness of approach was in this context a form of courtesy.

Now that her first experience of putting on a play is over, Joan has taken to claiming that the daily obligation to spend time with other people is what most exhausted her about the life of the theatre. And yet as we experimented through two workshop periods in tiny 50-seat spaces with the brilliant New York actor Linda Emond reading the role, I did not notice our playwright many times choosing to forgo that obligation. On the contrary. Most days she managed to get to rehearsal well before the director, and to leave well after. Far from shrinking away, she became friends with everyone in the room.

When, in March 2007, we moved our finished production into the Booth Theatre to face our first audience, a small table was set up for her in the wings by the stage manager, Karen Armstrong. A check tablecloth was bought and onto it was put a small handwritten sign: Café Didion. I stumbled on an outlet on Ninth Avenue which sold superb fried chicken at a dollar a piece. I would take a box of pieces back and serve them with collard greens. Teas of scones, croissants and jam became part of our way of life.

Further, as the months had gone by, as workshops had merged into rehearsals, there was no tangential appeal, however lowly, which Joan had not been ready to answer. If there was a costume fitting, she was there. If I was discussing a detail of the set with my old colleague Bob Crowley, she was hovering. If an interview had to be given, it was Joan who volunteered. Although she is generally represented as shy and retiring – and although she herself encourages that characterisation – I noticed that she had not been slow to publicise her book, and now her play. At one point, unbelievably, she was trailing from one American city to another, with 48-hour returns to Manhattan in between: the most exhausting itinerary possible, not least for a woman in her seventies.

When I later remarked that a television film about Joan of which we had had high hopes, and with which we both had cooperated, had turned out disappointing, she replied, 'No good deed goes unpunished', but seemed not at all put out. Something was going on here beyond the usual lame rituals of encouraging people to buy books or come to the box office.

The best directors are invariably the most collegiate. Joan's desire to throw herself into the novel process of theatre was, for me, an unforeseen bonus. I was happy to work with her always at my side. We agreed on most things – on the ravishing abstractions of Bob's designs, on the formal beauty of Brigitte Lacombe's photographs and on the subtlety of Jean Kalman's lighting. But most of all we agreed on the casting. The literal-minded may have found it hard to understand why we wanted Vanessa Redgrave. She's so tall, they said. She's so English. (Outside the marquee, Philip Roth looked at the poster and murmured to me, not without a trace of envy, 'Ah yes, Princess Margaret as Joan Didion.') But Vanessa had long been part of Joan's life, a country member at least of the Malibu club. She understood the territory. We cast the actor we knew would perform the play best, the one with the most profound access to the feelings of the character and a consummate flair for the phrasing of the words. The whole world knows Vanessa as an emotional master, but as a stylist she is nonpareil.

The overwhelming two-minute ovation which greeted the first sight of her on her return to the New York stage did no more than express publicly what Joan and I had throughout been feeling in private.

Of course, by creating two formidable works drawn from some overlapping subject matter, Joan resigned herself to passing through a few air pockets on the literary skyways. There were some people who had admired the book who could not find the same authority in the play. But, interestingly, there were just as many who had thought themselves in some way above the book who were willing to admit to being far more moved in the theatre. In his collected letters, Ted Hughes writes that nine-tenths of poetic criticism tells you more about the critic than it does about the poem. George Santayana intended something similar, remarking that when he read newspapers, he formed perhaps a new opinion of the newspaper, but seldom a new opinion of the subject discussed.

However, in this case I did have a rare sympathy for anyone whose job was to explicate such quicksilver work to others. I had noticed when I wrote *The Blue Room* that professional critics, faced with a play so rooted in the extremes and hypocrisies of the bedroom, found it hard to be honest, to speak in a level tone of voice. But if sex is hard to write about, imagine then the task of writing about death. Discussing death, we reveal something intimate, even shocking about ourselves.

The Year of Magical Thinking is at one level a character study, where the light thrown by tragedy remodels the Sacramento heroine in a different aspect. Those who claim that a monologue cannot, by definition, be a real play seem not to know that the journey we make to understanding our own position in the world can be one of the most dramatic of our lives. The play, in my head at least, sets off a thousand different reactions, not all of them the same at every performance. I've seen it fifty times. Yes, it's funny – funnier than audiences expect. But it's also bewildering. You find yourself wondering why someone so clever appears to be acting so stupid.

This, then, is why, when I look back on our time in New York, nothing in it seems more significant than the moment at which, somewhat late in the process, we asked ourselves why the play had been written at all. We were sitting in the Booth, probably at an afternoon rehearsal during the preview period, watching Vanessa up on the stage telling us once more about her moody Irish husband and her beautiful, volatile daughter. The author and director had one of those psychic moments at which two people think the same thing. Joan pointed one of her spidery fingers at the stalls. 'Wouldn't this be better,' she asked, 'if it were less about me? And more about them?' Next day, she inserted the blazing admonishment with which the play opens.

> This happened on December 30, 2003. That may seem
>   a while ago but it won't when it happens to you.

> And it will happen to you. The details will be different,
>   but it will happen to you.
> That's what I'm here to tell you.
> You see me on this stage, you sit next to me on a plane,
>   you run into me at dinner, you know what happened
>   to me.
> You don't want to think it could happen to you.

At a stroke, the play was turned from reminiscence into *Lehrstück*. By coming to the theatre, we could all begin to prepare ourselves for events which we hope to avoid but cannot. What had been a spectacle became a warning. An inward-looking play turned out. From then on, it flew.

(2008)

SARAH BERNHARDT

The Yale University Press Jewish Lives series is outstanding, with succinct biographies of interesting people like Peggy Guggenheim and Ben Hecht. But the coincidence of Robert Gottlieb's volume on Sarah Bernhardt being published at the same time as Simon Callow's My Life in Pieces *(Nick Hern Books) fired up my admiration for actors.*

What a pleasure! Suddenly there are a couple of first-rate books about acting. How often can that be said? Sure, the shelves of bookshops are always groaning with aspirational 'How To' manuals, aimed at suggestible students with rich parents. Such books generally turn out to be as much value to natural actors as a Masters and Johnson survey would have been to Tristan and Isolde. They fixate on technique without addressing purpose. Why be an actor in the first place? Publication of Simon Callow's collected arts journalism alongside a succinct, beautifully illustrated new biography of Sarah Bernhardt by Robert Gottlieb raises questions about what it is actors do, and why they are subject of such public distrust.

For a reader, the reaction to both books has been just as revealing as the books themselves. Simon Callow is rightly regarded as one of the best writer-actors we have. His range of knowledge is formidable, and he is as much at home defending Peter Ustinov, a once famous star who has fallen from view, as he is expanding on more familiar subjects like Cocteau, Stanislavsky or Micheál Mac Liammóir. And yet in the way some reviewers have reacted to the tone of his writing – nobody, after all, can question his expertise – there's been a muted strain of disapproval. First, not everyone cares for Callow's generosity and enthusiasm. They suspect such pleasure in achievement must imply a lack of discrimination. But second, they fear that he wants to drag the art of acting backwards from a stabilised comfort zone, underpinned by state subsidy, to make it larger and more heroic.

This is to misunderstand *My Life in Pieces*. This volume reads less like a plea for scale than a lament for mystery. Callow was drawn into the theatre by actors like Paul Scofield, who seemed not so much bigger than the rest of us as more tantalising and more unknowable. The usual put-down is to call Callow a hero-worshipper. But what's wrong with heroes, when they always turn out to be people who he believes know something he doesn't? Callow wants to learn and be moved by watching not just actors, but people whom he feels to be more profound and complicated than himself. Scofield is for Callow the supreme actor, because his essential gift, even in his harshest roles, was for intimating something secret, something almost beyond the spectator's reach. Pre-eminently as King Lear, Scofield seemed not just to comprehend the world's injury better than the audience, but also to carry its bruises deeper inside him. (It was the greatest male tragic performance I ever saw; Anthony Hopkins in *Pravda*, the greatest comic). But that particular sense of emotional wisdom put him in the company of a whole range of British stage actors of a certain experience – Alec Guinness, clearly, Maggie Smith, Denholm Elliott, and perhaps above all Irene Worth – who could suggest an internal life which they could make us long to understand.

For good or ill, it's not a common contemporary quality. Today, in a lot of British theatre, things could hardly be more different. Only occasionally – as in the draped expressiveness of Lesley Sharp's performance in Simon Stephens' *Harper Regan*, or when Penelope Wilton cut the still air with consonants as Hester in Rattigan's *The Deep Blue Sea* – do you see an actor setting out to refine gesture and stress with the aim of pulling you in. The sweatier fashion is for pushing interpretation out. Typically, the most praised performance of the age is Mark Rylance's as Johnny 'Rooster' Byron in Jez Butterworth's *Jerusalem*. It's an athletic feat, technically dazzling, and yet, like the Pompidou Centre, with all its gizzards showing on the outside. Not for a moment does Rylance try to involve you in his mystery, because elucidating mystery is not his aim, any more than it is for a gymnast or a great prop forward. No one watching can fail to be impressed with the effort. How on earth does any human being do that eight times a week? But, unlike when Bruno Ganz in *Downfall* drew on such a phenomenal level of technical expertise impersonating Hitler in the face of death, we are on this occasion watching a display, not an intimation. Ganz took you inside, Rylance keeps you out.

The conclusion from all this might well be that, on account of their sheltered lives – no war, no desolating hardship – present-day performers appear to have less trust in the idea that they are interesting in themselves than those who survived the rough knocks of the last mid-century. You might even argue that they suggest less because they have suffered less. But anyone lucky enough to spend ten minutes in the company of Ralph Fiennes or Richard Griffiths or Judi Dench would dispose of that theory. What is changing here is style, and the freedom of the actor to express within the play something which is both rooted in the action and the character but which also seems to take us beyond it. It was a parallel quality – of always being Sarah Bernhardt, and always connecting the audience to the unfathomable strangeness of being Bernhardt – to which critics of the nineteenth century's most famous actor objected. Yes, Bernhardt enjoyed international success playing Phèdre, playing Cleopatra, and especially playing Camille. But, in any role, even Hamlet, they said, she was always Bernhardt.

Anyone who imagines that in the twenty-first century actors enjoy an inappropriate level of acclaim will read of Bernhardt's life with some disbelief. Fame was on a level which few Hollywood stars can now emulate. By the time Bernhardt died in 1923, the presumed model for the great actress Berma in Proust's *À la Recherche du temps perdu* ('So Berma's interpretation was, around Racine's work, a second work, quickened also by the breath of genius'), half a million people waited to watch her cortège go through the streets of Paris. But, reading Gottlieb, you may recognise from responses to the nature of her life, its extraordinary provocation of gossip, speculation and rumour, something of the same resentment which marks out so many journalistic attitudes to actors today. In particular, you will stumble on the identical snobbish conviction, common to high- and lowbrow newspapers alike, that actors need to be slapped down when they dare to leave the playhouse or the cinema and enter the national discourse.

Bernhardt was of course not above doing things to attract attention. If you habitually go to bed in a coffin, and you also maintain a private menagerie of three dogs, a parrot, a monkey, a cheetah, an alligator, a boa constrictor and seven chameleons, the chances are that people will talk. But there was in the sheer nastiness of the objections both to her race and her gender – when she played *La Sorcière* in Roman Catholic Montreal, there were cries of 'Kill the Jewess' – a distinctly modern note of hostility. When we learn that in Paris cafés it was claimed that the reason for the special charge of her greatness in the theatre was her inability to achieve orgasm away from it – 'She doesn't have a clitoris, she has a corn,' said one wag, while Marie Colombier called her 'an untuned piano, an Achilles vulnerable everywhere except in the right place' – then we appear to have picked up a 150-year-old copy of *Private Eye*.

Bernhardt's cheery promiscuity, born out of her lifelong habit of routinely sleeping with her leading men, usually in the dressing room, sometimes before and sometimes after performances, and thereby building up what Gottlieb calls 'her human menagerie', was indeed a vital part of her legend. When one of her younger lovers, Lou Tellegen, later published his memoirs *Women Have Been Kind,* it was Dorothy Parker who suggested that the words 'Of Dumb' should have been added to the title. But it was Bernhardt's active participation in decisive historical events which did even more than her acting to seal her reputation.

Working from the same motives which attract such vituperative scorn towards Angelina Jolie and Sean Penn, she chose, during the Franco-Prussian War, to turn the Odéon

Theatre into a military hospital, ministering with great effectiveness and dedication to the injured, the maimed and the dying whom she laid out 'in the lobbies, in the auditorium, in the wings, [and] in the dressing rooms'. Having made a fortune out of repeatedly feigning death on stage, she turned out to be fearless in the face of it under non-theatrical bombardment. But, just as important, her passionate advocacy of Captain Dreyfus's cause over twenty years later in the 1890s not only split her own family down the middle but also stoked her notoriety in the right-wing press. In that seminal French dispute, which helped trigger so many of the shattering events of the subsequent century, she took the side of the good and paid the price.

'The great actress is with the Jews against the army,' ran one headline.

Of the nature of her acting itself it's hard to be sure. The brief excerpts you may find on YouTube will tell you little. For two hundred years every generation of actor has claimed to be more 'real' and therefore less artificial than the previous. It can hardly be true of all of them or we would long have passed way beyond even the behaviourist point represented by Greta Gerwig's trademark mumbling. Hailed as fresh and revolutionary when she set out, Bernhardt lived and worked long enough to be condemned as old-fashioned in Duse's shadow. But anyone with my own prejudices is going to take note of what one observer called 'her talent for endowing immobility with excitement' – as good a definition of a certain kind of great stage acting as I've heard. Bernhardt was, in Gottlieb's judicious summary, 'a child of the Romantic movement, and her theatre was the theatre of feelings, of rebellion, of the Self . . . Her exaggerated thinness, her pale colouring, her exotic face, and her poetic charm set her off from every other actress . . .' Little wonder, then, that these characteristics left her a miserable member of an ensemble – she had little success, for instance, at the Comédie-Française – and best able to lead a company from the front, on her own terms and nobody else's. She was happiest on tour.

It is no coincidence that the most memorable and prophetic description of her came from someone fastidious, who was both awed and repelled by her make-up. Henry James saw Bernhardt for the first time playing, as always, in her own language in London in 1880, and predicted extravagant success for her in the United States. Calling her 'a child of her age – of her moment' who had known how to profit by the idiosyncrasies of her time, James went on to note that 'The trade of a celebrity, pure and simple, had been invented, I think, before she came to London; if it had not been, it is certain she would have discovered it. She has in a supreme degree what the French call the *génie de la réclame* – the advertising genius . . .'

There is in that resentful mix of admiration and dislike a note which anyone who works today in the performing arts will recognise at once. Since Bernhardt's time, acting and celebrity have become so intertwined that it's hard to remember that some of the world's most famous names do a job of work, and do it well. Almost alone among film critics, David Thomson in his reviews and in his *Biographical Dictionary of Film* (1975) writes with informed warmth about actors, often seeing the world their way round and crediting them with the dignity of their own choices. He is as discerning at noticing a good actor in a small role as he is at analysing the power of a star. Uniquely, Thomson discusses a film as if its defining flavour may just as well come from an actor as from a director. When he remarks that Cary Grant, alone among film actors, had the ability to be charming and sinister, not in succession, but in the exact same moment, Thomson is showing that very same sensitivity to mystery Simon Callow seeks to illuminate.

Meanwhile, in a world away from pretending to be someone else, actors are still, after all this time, assumed to be not quite legitimate when they express opinions on anything except how to find the stage door after dark. However easy it is to think of approved establishment names – I could pluck a dozen out of the air and still not reach the letter C – who spend their lives proclaiming things more stupid and downright wrong than anything even Mel Gibson ever said, yet, under cartel rules, it is guaranteed that their membership of the reserve professions – politics and journalism, journalism and politics – entitles them to immunity. They remain secure, exempt from the contempt doled out, say, to Vanessa Redgrave, to Kylie Minogue, or, in her day, to Sarah Bernhardt. The relationship of public opinion to professional pretence remains as flatteringly complicated as it was in nineteenth-century France. People fear actors because they tell them something about themselves.

(2010)

THE GRIEVANCES OF
TERENCE RATTIGAN

Of course, you must expect it. In right-wing times, right-wing art flourishes. In the London theatre, the Donmar Warehouse has prospered by seeking out the Christian mystic playwrights of the last century like T. S. Eliot and Enid Bagnold, while a journey through the West End today offers almost no new plays of any intelligence. At the cinema, *The King's Speech* has swept all before it, while the most interesting British film of last year, *The Arbor*, being about women on a Bradford council estate, has barely been seen. On television, the nation sits down every Sunday to an Edwardian fiction, *Downton Abbey*, in which the upper classes are revealed, to the astonishment of the grateful viewer, to be quaintly caring about the welfare of the lower. But in this national festival of reaction, the attempt not just to extol but also to redeem from martyrdom the eminent playwright Terence Rattigan represents the most intriguing cultural rejig of all.

Contrary to almost everything you may have read in this centenary year of his birth, Rattigan is a dramatist who has never been far from the public eye. For as long as I can remember audiences have admired what John Osborne described as his 'craftmanship like a carriage clock . . . and so he gets ten out of ten, quite rightly'. There have been excellent revivals of his major works, especially on television. I saw Virginia McKenna being a memorable Hester in *The Deep Blue Sea* in 1974, and

I have never forgotten Alan Badel's Arctic chill as Sir Robert Morton in a 1977 *Winslow Boy*.

It is true that thanks to the revelatory performance of Penelope Wilton, again in *The Deep Blue Sea*, this time at the Almeida in 1993, a new generation marvelled at how potent Rattigan could be when he addressed his most profound subject: man's and woman's helplessness in the face of their own true character. It was the eerie way in which Wilton managed to be both perfectly in period and at the same time contemporary that made this the definitive Rattigan production. But, even then, it did not seem as if we were being introduced to a play whose outline – woman gives everything up for sex – was not familiar already.

Why then is it essential to the temper of the times to pretend that Rattigan, of all playwrights, has been uniquely hard done by? It has become a commonplace of commentary to turn him into some sort of public-school victim whose fall from grace can be put down to nasty goings-on initiated by yobs at the Royal Court and at Stratford East in the 1950s. In this seigneurial rewriting of history, the long-delayed opening up of the British stage to working-class voices in two small auditoria on either side of London took place at the expense of a solid craftsman whose skilful celebrations of English middle-class reticence fell unfairly out of favour.

There are so many misconceptions in this standard narrative that it is hard to know where to begin. For once in theatrical history, it is impossible to blame the critics. If we are to believe, as is claimed, that Rattigan was disheartened into silence by some indifferent reviews for his starry plays about Horatio Nelson and T. E. Lawrence, let us take a look, please, at the far more brutal treatment handed out to those very same playwrights – Bond, Arden and Osborne – who in right-wing mythology are supposed to have supplanted him.

Years on from it all, our dramatic ecology is much as it has always been: apolitical formalist experiment and classical revival jostling in pleasant diversity alongside vehicles for jetted-in Hollywood stars and evenings of musical uplift. The glories of the British theatre remain the brilliance of its actors and the vibrancies of its small spaces. At no point have long-dead revolutionaries from Sloane Square and Stratford East looked like taking over the show.

Those of us who lived through the Thatcher years will remember how, for the first time, the powerful and successful were encouraged to develop an ugly vein of grievance. To the beaming approval of the prime minister, fabulously wealthy business folk took to telling us how little appreciated they were, and how intolerable it was to carry an equal burden of taxation and misunderstanding. With Cameron in charge this wheedling tone of self-righteous privilege has come back into public discourse. The attempt to turn Rattigan into a martyr is simply its cultural equivalent.

The truth is that Rattigan was inconsistent, like most of us. Alongside some other lasting plays and films, he achieved two unarguable masterpieces, *The Browning Version* and *The Deep Blue Sea*, both of which show that his attitude to the value of emotional reticence was a great deal more ambivalent than is generally made out. He also, God help us, dreamt up audience punishments like *The V.I.P.s*. If you want to die on a hill named *The Prince and the Showgirl*, good luck to you.

During the preparation for Benedict Cumberbatch's BBC Four documentary to be shown this summer, I was asked a question which was far more insulting than anything Rattigan's enemies ever flung at him. The researcher wanted to know if it had not been for the emergence of the angry young men whether Rattigan would have gone on to write many more great plays. I tried to explain that most writers, at most times, are doing their best. Their success or failure in mining their imagination depends principally on the limits of that imagination. If they have any courage or experience at all, they are unlikely to be put off by the irrationality of the artistic stock exchange. A playwright goes to work in all weather.

Unfortunately, driving around in a Rolls-Royce with a personalised numberplate TR100 is not going to change the mix of ingredients necessary to writing more than one good play. A certain blind stubbornness will be among them. Rattigan knew that. But as Peggy Ramsay wrote, 'Once an author has become successful and famous, it becomes more difficult to speak the truth, and this is why people like Rattigan become bloodless.' Rattigan must indeed have suffered by not being invited to be part of Laurence Olivier's nascent National Theatre in 1963. But if you must write, you must. If fashion put you off, you'd never write at all.

In *The Browning Version*, Rattigan wrote a play in which a crabbed and implicitly homosexual classics teacher, by a display of clever masochism, manages to persuade an attractive games master to abandon an affair with his wife and to come instead on a holiday with him in Devon. The fact that no production of *The Browning Version* ever dares to make this theme plain

– or, worse, doesn't want to – says something about how we haven't moved on in our sexual attitudes as much as we pretend. We are determined to see Rattigan as a victim, when in fact he could, in art at least, portray a shrewd manipulator who uses his suffering as a discreet form of blackmail over others apparently more powerful. Nothing wrong with that. The tyranny of the weak is a fascinating subject for drama. But the fact that a crop of Rattigan revivals is being hailed in some circles as the realignment of the whole cultural globe back onto its natural axis says more about us, I'm afraid, than it does about him.

(2010)

THE PAINTER, PATRICK CAULFIELD

My favourite photograph of Patrick Caulfield was taken by Jillian Edelstein in 1999. The artist is sitting low in a battered brown-leather chair, wearing blue worker's overalls which are splashed with paints of many colours. His hand is resting below his lip, and he's looking straight at the camera, as if he had nothing to fear from its scrutiny. On his face is an expression, both amused and impenetrable, which anyone who met him will recognise at once to be characteristic. But above all you can't help noticing how handsome Patrick is.

The looks of an artist ought not to be a factor in judging their art. But just as it's hard to disentangle the work of Van Gogh, Lee Miller or Modigliani from their extraordinary appearances – Giacometti looks like a Giacometti, Rembrandt like a Rembrandt, Paolozzi like a Paolozzi and Bacon like a Bacon – so Patrick's own physical serenity seems to provide at least a parallel to his work. I've known very few people with such a profound sense of self-certainty. Artists in most disciplines are by habit neurotic, fretting either about their inadequacies or the unfairness of how they're being received. Unforgotten slights and missed opportunities loom large, especially in conversation. But Patrick belongs among those very few who not only know what they want to do, but who appear not to care what anyone thinks of it.

On one occasion, I was one of the first few people to be shown a painting – of a leg of lamb – over which he'd just spent the previous two months. He took me into his studio and took away the dishcloth with which he'd covered it. As it happened, I loved it, and he was delighted. But he left me feeling that he wouldn't have minded if I hadn't. It was no good asking him where you might get to see so many of his old pictures. He'd given them to his dealer and thereafter lost interest. 'Where are they, Patrick?' 'No idea. Don't know.'

I first got to know him through my wife, Nicole. I'd already noticed that most artists I met deferred to him. The very fact that he did not attract fellow-painterly jealousy tells you something about him. If someone asked Howard Hodgkin or Paula Rego which of their colleagues they most admired, they would usually say, 'Patrick', as if his was the one name everyone could agree on. If you asked artists why he wasn't better known – as famous, say, as Freud or Hockney – they'd say, 'Because he's too good.'

The lazy way of looking at his work is to say that it's painting about painting. The way he deploys colour and the way he mixes together objects and landscapes in differing styles is taken to be some sort of comment on the arbitrariness of representation. And it's true that in many of his pictures he does seem to be seeking to lay bare the definitive differences between one dimension and three. But in my own view he's doing this not just as play, but to a purpose: he wants to show us the haunting unknowability of the environment in which human beings have to spend their lives. Was there ever a major painter who painted so few people? Even when he'd send me an occasional painting done for my birthday, or for a first night, only my arm would appear, perhaps behind a curtain. Or just a curtain. Or a spotlight. Certainly no sign of me. Even Juan Gris, you will notice, painted to the nines, is left suspended by Patrick in starkly hostile surroundings. And was there ever anyone who portrayed so much food, while themselves being so uninterested in eating?

I'm not quite sure why he and I got on so well, though I suspect that the fact that neither of us knew anything about each other's artistic past played a large part in it. We both valued wit as one of the highest human accomplishments. I certainly did not share his taste for whisky. By the time of day when we met up, he'd already have done his regular stint of morning painting, plus his steady hours on a stool in the Belsize Tavern, and he'd be ready to talk about anything. He also was formidable when in companionable silence.

We shared a common passion for uncontemporary cinema, and I loved introducing him to Renoir films he didn't know, because I was so sure he'd understand them. On the other hand, he remained unable to convince me in return that *Ulzana's Raid* (1972), a western with Burt Lancaster, was the greatest film ever made. In the last days, when cancer of the jaw meant that he couldn't speak, he would pass beautifully written little notes across. One, unforgettably, read: 'Forgive me. It's six o'clock in the evening, and this time always makes me sad.' On another occasion, he asked, on a note, what I was up to. Not wanting to say, I replied 'Fiddling around.' Back came his written reply: 'I never fiddle around.'

By the time the drink really kicked in, at dinner, say, or after, you would see flashes of a stuttering anger which could bring an evening to a halt – caused by his own inability to express in language thoughts and feelings he sets out so eloquently in paint. I was always aware that he was ruthless – ruthless as only an artist can be. It did not surprise me when the late impetus of his work was to strip away. He revelled more and more in unoccupied rooms, abandoned objects and lone exit signs. Latency became his subject. The world was charged, but unwilling to reveal itself. He'd always preferred to paint the record player than the band. One of his greatest pictures, after all, is of a stereo deck. But as the years went by, the formidable technical skills and the mastery of preparation became even more perfect, while the subject matter became ever more ambiguous. By the end, he could shock you with a pair of doors.

Ultimately, that's his gift – to charge the canvas with feeling by methods which remain oblique. Our friendship was the same. He is buried in Highgate Cemetery opposite Ralph Richardson. It seems appropriate. Two people beneath whose impeccable, everyday surface lay unbearable sadness.

(2013)

MAD MEN

I wrote twice about Mad Men, *once in 2010 and then again in 2012. I suffered that common derangement when you love something or someone: you imagine that no one else understands the object of your love.*

In a hilariously combative interview in the *Evening Standard* last March, the best-selling author Lee Child argued the superiority of thrillers over any other kind of fiction. The problem with the literary novel was that it was too easy. Child, he said, could knock off a Martin Amis in three weeks. The only literary writer for whom he had any respect was Ian McEwan, because McEwan was at least trying to 'put a suspense dynamic into an intelligent, intellectual novel'. So-called serious writers 'don't quite get it' because they're usually too fastidious to accept how simple the formula is. 'You ask or imply a question at the beginning of a book and you absolutely self-consciously withhold the answer. It does feel cheap and meretricious but it absolutely works.'

'Cheap and meretricious' may seem an unlikely way to describe the programme which is persuading many of us that the future of American film belongs on television, but anyone contemplating Lee Child's prescription is going to hear eight bells ringing when they settle down to the fourth series of *Mad Men*. Once it had been established, very early on, that the masterly advertising executive Don Draper had a past identity to which he didn't admit, everything has followed effortlessly, both in plot and in theme. The man's a fake. But who is he? The murky and rather conventional flashback sequences which have sketched in a rural upbringing and funny business during the war are admittedly the only clumsy elements in what has otherwise been thirty-nine hours of superbly achieved production. The Gatsby question has provided a framework which has held the series steady from beginning to end. But it has also licensed the writers to wander into the lives of at least twelve other equally dodgy characters without ever making the audience feel they are leaving home. The series' extraordinary freedom is a product of its discipline. Hanging plot lines are like brushstrokes in a picture which is all the richer by not being tidied up.

It needs courage to withhold, and withholding is what this series is all about. Feature films in the English language seem to obsess more and more on only one thing at a time – they concentrate on their given subject with a kind of furious, exhausting dullness. But in *Mad Men*, nothing is dwelt on very long and, as in life, lots of things happen at once. It's typical of the writers' complicating techniques that when, at the climax of three series, Don Draper drives home to find his wife Betty has finally opened his desk drawer and come upon evidence of his previous self, he meanwhile has another woman waiting for him in the car outside.

Even when facing the crisis of his life, our hero's mind can't help, partly at least, being on something else.

Critics of the series have tried to suggest that what we are watching here is fancy soap – the lives and loves of a group of people in a shared milieu. They echo the complaints made against contemporary novels like Jonathan Franzen's *The Corrections*, whose popularity critics love to resent. But no soap I ever watched has the governing metaphor of authenticity. If Don Draper has no idea what he really thinks and feels, who does? Who exactly are these people? And is anything they say or do real – to themselves, or to us? As someone who likes never to spoil their pleasure by reading about the things they most enjoy, I have tried to avoid commentary. But whenever I have seen *Mad Men* described I have been mystified. Why on earth do people call it a satire? And why is its real subject assumed to be the 1960s?

Of course, it may be hard to imagine *Mad Men* being written without the influence of the great novelist Richard Yates, the author of *The Easter Parade* and *Revolutionary Road*, or perhaps even more closely of Sloan Wilson, who wrote *The Man in the Gray Flannel Suit*. The depiction of a certain moment in professional New York is presumably accurate. But surely the reason that the alcohol, the sexism, the insecurity, the duplicity, the bare-faced lying and the status anxiety at work have taken such hold on the public imagination is because they so perfectly match our own experiences. Has anything changed? Isn't the whole joy of *Mad Men*'s immaculate recreation of one way of life that it reminds us of another – namely, our own? Having recently spent eight months researching the banking business, I can't say I saw women in the City of London in 2009 treated all that differently from how the men treated Peggy, Betty or Joan in 1963. The cocktail cabinet wasn't exactly jammed shut either.

And as for satire . . . the triumph of the series is it doesn't waste time on the predictable business of making fun of advertising. Satire's been done before, and often badly. No, for once, here is a group of professional people who resemble us, both in the unlikeliness of what they have to do and the seriousness with which they set about it. They use their flashes of occasional inspiration to make possible something which may or may not be worthy of them.

What's being identified – and only occasionally mocked – is the mixture of fear, swagger and resignation with which so many employees in Anglo-Saxon businesses now swerve along assault courses designed by distant owners with whom they have no particular relationship, and who, in return, have no interest in their well-being. In Richard Yates's account, advertising is represented as trivial and uninvolving, an unworthy way for war veterans to pass the time, and therefore only a background to their personal crises. In *Mad Men*, it's the way they work their crises through.

It's a splendid coincidence that *Mad Men* will relaunch in this country just one day before M&C's splashy Chelsea party to celebrate forty years of the Saatchi brothers. It's not noted in routine hagiographies of Margaret Thatcher, supposedly a rock of purpose and integrity, that she was the woman who made government and advertising more or less interchangeable. *Mad Men*, at its most basic, plugs into the theme of class which powers so much great American art. Like *Some Came Running*, *The Godfather*, or *A Place in the Sun*, or indeed its immediate progenitor *The Sopranos*, it features aspirational characters who think they want to move up through society, but who are haunted by the feeling that gain is loss. The sanctuary of the suburb is a poor trade for the vitality of the street. They thought they wanted to advance and all they've done is retreat. By gaining respectability, they have lost authenticity.

When, ten years ago, I wrote that 'The classic American hero sits at the window of his or her study with a book in his hand, or in a big mansion with a cocktail in his or her hand, wondering whether he or she mightn't have been better off not making the journey', I might have been foreseeing something resembling *Mad Men*. But, in fact, its special achievement has been to go one step further. *Mad Men* shows a world, not so very far from that of our coalescent prime minister 'Dave' Cameron, in which everyone can get away with being who they claim to be, rather than who they are. Can anyone truly tell me if Dave is Dick or Don? Does even he know?

In all this, it has been the writing which has been the star. The recent English-language publication of François Truffaut's last interview finds him regretting the dismal consequences of trying to turn regular film directors into auteurs. The intention of the *nouvelle vague*, he said, had been 'more personal films', but the results were films which were, in fact, 'more than personal: they became narcissistic'. Gradually, Truffaut said, he had himself returned 'to a narrative tradition based more on observation and synthesis than subjectivity and self-exploration'. The lessons learnt by Truffaut in twenty years still haven't been absorbed by Anglo-American cinema in sixty. *Mad Men* has auteurs, all right. They're not the directors. They're the boys and girls who write it.

(2010)

MAD MEN 5

Hare Krishna, LSD, and shacking up: in series 5, *Mad Men* is decisively on the move. For so long rooted in the early 1960s, this most literary of TV series is now schlepping up the decade to take root in the world of Tom Wolfe and even of Hunter S. Thompson. Let's hope Kate Millett and Betty Friedan are lying in wait round the corner to blow things even more dramatically apart. And whereas our own *Downton Abbey* was happy to deal with the entire First World War in a couple of episodes, the characters in *Mad Men* 5 are condemned to absorb every painful indignity that generational change in the mid-1960s had to offer.

Once so cool, Don Draper and company now look decidedly un-so.

In his film *This Is 40*, Judd Apatow has his own children defending the vitality of the event-driven *Lost* by comparing it with their father's beloved *Mad Men*, which, the children say, is nothing but 'people sitting in rooms, talking and smoking'. It's true of this fifth foray, which is admittedly a bit slow to get going, that you can't always tell whether its pervasive malaise is accidental or intentional. Is it deliberate that, in Jon Hamm's unsettling performance, Don Draper seems diminished by his determination to be grimly faithful to his new wife? And is it chance that the soul of the series seems to have migrated to Roger Sterling, who, as brought to you by the glittering John

Slattery, has turned into a fully fledged Jaques, celebrating each of his own seven ages with a wilder sexual anarchy and an even deeper despair? Hey, is that the great Julia Ormond, discarded after a couple of episodes, apparently invited in just to give oral sex in a French accent to Roger?

Mad Men's regular alternation between costive offices and costive bedrooms makes for an uneasy watch. Whisky and cigarettes were never the subject of this series. They were always just the dressing, like fans in Restoration plays, or guns in Bogart movies. What's at stake here is the promiscuous gene itself, and the restlessness of capitalism, the way dissatisfaction is inseparable from attainment. 'This is the best it will ever get,' Peggy tells Megan after they clinch the Heinz contract. Christina Hendricks has Joan become even more buffed and gleaming as soon as she's ordered her husband out of her life. The colour block of her clothes gets ever more primary. At each moment in *Mad Men*, the characters have it and they don't.

You may think the whole enterprise is getting a little self-conscious, as if the people who make *Mad Men* have read too many articles about *Mad Men*. At one point, there's even a dinner with a Canadian Marxist who, God help us, has a critique. But isn't that what the poet tells us happens to good work? It becomes its admirers.

TV series are an oddball art form because the audience may well have its say before the artist is finished, and that can affect the tone. (Imagine anyone trying to stand at Francis Bacon's elbow. Or Virginia Woolf's.) If you look at it, as I prefer to do, in a box set, all in one go, you are bound to notice that each of the characters is finding middle age hard. Betty's getting fat, and Peggy's getting furious. Everyone's making the same discovery, that prosperity has its own distinctive melancholy. Perhaps it was more fun for us, and for them, when they knew less. But it's not untrue.

(2012)

FINGERS CROSSED: THE LIFE
OF JIMMY SAVILE

In the United States, no gun is fired and no bird falls to the ground without the incident at once being appropriated by both sides as ammunition in a culture war. Democratic politics having been finally wrestled to the ground by big business and big finance, the most bitter field of controversy has shifted from how we're governed to how we behave. The smallest incident, it seems, is proof of an existing argument, one way or another. Up till recently in the United Kingdom we've been spared a great deal of this mindless back and forth, but the recent revelation of Jimmy Savile's vile character has brought signs that things are heading the same way. Traders in opinion have had an orgy throwing Savile against the wall to see what sticks.

To entrenched analysts on one side, Savile is represented as the embodiment of deep cultural misogyny. Throughout his life he referred to the women he violated as 'it'. In the view of the left, he is a Conservative con man who dined yearly at Chequers, a shameless Tartuffe to the royal family, and, disgracefully, a celebrity all too ready to blackmail individual members of the Prison Officers Association to prevent strikes, after his appointment to the Broadmoor Task Force was approved by Edwina Currie at the Department of Health. 'Attaboy!' wrote Currie in her diary, when Savile told her of his plans for the hospital. 'Jimmy is truly a great Briton,' added Mrs Thatcher, 'a stunning example of opportunity Britain, a dynamic example of enterprise

Britain, and an inspiring example of responsible Britain.' But to polemicists on the right, looking for corroboration of what they already believe, Savile is, to the contrary, shocking proof of the moral downside of the new freedoms of the 1960s, and an indictment of two handy ideological targets, which may therefore, they hope, be tarnished by association: the National Health Service and the BBC. A hapless medical expert who argued in the *Guardian* that Savile wasn't evil but more likely a victim of bad parenting was immediately torn to pieces in the correspondence columns by the readers.

The best hope for the publication of a substantial book by the journalist who spent most time with Savile, and who interviewed him frequently, is that stale controversy may at last be refreshed by the application of a few facts. The portrait painted by Dan Davies might as well be that of a murderer as of a rapist. Born in Leeds in 1926 as the last of seven children to a ferocious mother, Agnes, who was to remain the sole love of his life, Savile was a solitary child who played alone. When sent down the mines as a Bevin boy, he realised that by turning up in a suit, working naked, then washing his hands and feet while at the bottom of the pit, he might come back up to leave the mine after a day's work as immaculate as when he arrived. In his own words, 'The effect was electric . . . I didn't do it for any reason, I just realised that going back clean would freak people out, and it did. Underneath the clothes I was black as night. But I realised that being a bit odd meant that there could be a payday.'

Having stumbled on what Davies calls the power of odd-ness, Savile was exhilarated to discover he could compound his power by becoming a disc jockey. At once he relished the feeling of control, allowing people to dance, fast or slow, only as and when he wanted. He loved what he took to calling 'the effect'. 'That's the thing that triggered me off and sustained me for the rest of my days.' By the time he became a manager of Mecca dance halls, first in Ilford, then in Manchester, he was developing a distinctive mix of gangster boasting, financial greed, and abuse of both sexes, often underage, while moving smoothly on to a career in television. This time, the 'effect' of his TV debut was immediate. When he returned to the dance hall to find people queuing round the block, he took special pleasure in them falling a step back, impressed, as he walked by. 'I thought, "Fucking hell, this is like having the keys to the Bank of England."'

Throughout the book it is presented as paradox that Savile, the best-known presenter of television programmes for young people, hated children. But it would be truer to say he hated people. He had no interest in relationships. 'I just don't have those feelings with another human being.' Self-evidently he hated women, on whom he sought to leave a violent and degrading stain, throwing them out of his Rolls-Royce if, during sex, they threatened to gag on its leatherwork. But, friendless and competitive, he wasn't crazy about men either, unless, like Prince Charles – who Princess Diana said regarded Savile as his mentor – they were in a position to make him yet more powerful.

As an intelligent man with an IQ said to be 150, Savile realised that if he could get tame policemen on his side by a mixture of bribery and flattery, he would be able to bluff his way in the face of the accusations which would inevitably begin to mount up. 'Why tell the truth', he asked, 'when you can get away with a lie?' Briefly called in as a suspect in the case of the Yorkshire Ripper, he had, he said, 'more front than Blackpool'. His technique for dealing with his victims was always to keep on the move. 'If anyone makes demands, they don't make them twice, pal, because they get the sack after the first time.' In a life roiling with sinister self-knowledge, nothing is more chilling than his declaration: 'There is no end of uses to a motor caravan.'

In normal circumstances, anyone who declared that the five days they spent alone with their mother's coffin were the happiest of their life – 'Once upon a time I had to share her with other people . . . But when she was dead, she was all mine' – would be subject to public scrutiny. So would somebody whose first reaction after quadruple bypass surgery was to grope the attendant nurse's breast. But by then Savile had pulled off the trick of seeming to make his surface weirdness part of what he called his 'charismatic package'. 'Nobody can be frightened of me. It would be beneath anyone's dignity to be frightened of someone dressed like this.' The popular press, always boastful of its fearlessness, was scared off. In the words of one Metropolitan Police Commander, 'He groomed a nation.' In his own words, 'I am a man what knows everything but says nothing.'

As he moved to consolidate his position and to work for the knighthood which he believed would make him untouchable, he took to raising vast sums of money for charity, most especially for a Spinal Injuries Unit at Stoke Mandeville.

His first question on arriving in any town was to ask where the hospital was. This was not just because a hospital offered sexual pickings and a captive audience for his ceaseless self-glorying monologues. Nor was it wholly because he needed the immunity which came from apparent respectability. Most important of all, he believed that the day would come when he would have to offer his good works as some mitigation against a final reckoning.

Apart from his mother, God is the only other supporting character in Savile's story, the only one who is granted more than a walk-on part. 'When I'm holding somebody that has just died, I'm filled with a tremendous love and envy. They've left behind their problems, they've made the journey. If somebody were to tell me tonight I wouldn't wake up in the morning, it would fill me with tremendous joy. Sometimes I can't wait.' Savile does not belong among the amoral heroes of Patricia Highsmith, disposing of people without remorse in a meaningless universe. Rather, he inhabits the driven world of Graham Greene, where the protagonist is in a lurid and sweaty argument with his maker, trying to pile up credit points to balance the final ledger against what he knows full well to be his sins. If the definition of a psychopath is someone who does not understand his own depravity, Savile is, to the consternation of medical apologists, the very opposite. He always carried the rosary the Pope had given him. On his deathbed, he was found with his fingers crossed.

In his book *God'll Fix It*, which collects his thoughts on matters religious, Savile offers a weaselly line of defence, claiming that everyone's true identity is in hock to the desires they are given and over which they can hope to have no control. The machine of the body which God has lent you may cause you to err, but nothing is finally your fault. 'It could be that the person arriving at the judgement seat had been given a body prone to excesses because the glands dictated that he should be more than was really normal.' He defends Broadmoor's inhabitants as 'more unlucky than bad', and argues that 'There's no point asking about that dark night . . . when something terrible happened because it wasn't them doing it. It was someone else using their body.' When asked if he has been following the Myra Hindley story he replies enigmatically, 'I am the Myra Hindley story.'

Like many Roman Catholics, he is concerned to make a good death – it's one of the most important things in his life – but at no point is he ever known to have given a moment's thought to the tormented deaths waiting for those whose lives he has ruined. Even in guilt, the drama is always about him. By the time he has been encouraged by his admirers to lead a peace march across Northern Ireland and to claim that he has been mooted as a potential intermediary between Begin and Sadat to reconcile warring parties in the Middle East, Savile's messiah complex has taken up every inch of space in his head. A stretcher-bearer at Leeds General Hospital commented on the award of his OBE: 'They often say he's a bit of a twit. Us, we say he's a bit of a bloody saint.'

There is nobody in the world who wants to read a bad book about Jimmy Savile, and there may well, for understandable reasons, be a limit to the number of people who want to read an outstanding one. Davies scarcely puts a foot wrong, interweaving Savile's story with a detailed account of how the

BBC's dysfunctional news department managed in 2011 both to suppress the scoop of Savile's offences and then, unbelievably, to further mishandle the admission of that suppression. The only errors of tone occur when the author obtrudes himself in the manner of self-conscious literary reportage, gussying the narrative up with needless speculation about his own personal motives for his longstanding obsession with his subject. We don't care.

If the book is less depressing than you might anticipate, it's because the act of biography itself here seems noble. So far 450 people have made allegations of sexual abuse against Savile. Across 28 police areas in England and Wales, he is known to have committed 214 criminal offences in 50 years. There are 31 allegations of rape, half of them against minors, and Dame Janet Smith's independent review at the BBC is believed to be about to claim that up to 1,000 young people may have been abused by Savile in the Corporation's dressing rooms. All religions rely on the notion of redemption, but the only redeeming feature of Savile's life is that he has posthumously lucked into such a clear-eyed and morally conscientious biographer. Prince Charles once wrote, 'Nobody will ever know what you have done for this country, Jimmy.' They do now.

(2014)

LILACS OUT OF THE DEADLAND:
JOE PAPP

For a long time Joe Papp was just a voice on the telephone. To understand our long relationship – which began scrappy but deepened into something mutually intense and valuable – you have to know that I wrote my first full-length play when I was twenty-three. I had enjoyed a hair-raising relationship with the American director who had staged its London premiere in 1970. This luckless fellow had managed to survive the formal revolt of the three English actresses who refused to go on spending their rehearsals playing ball games. They had appealed to the boss of Hampstead Theatre to be allowed to start performing the text. So it was rather surprising to find that this same director, careless of his ordeal, had tucked *Slag* under his arm on the plane back home and given it to a man who, on account of *Hair*, was recognised as the most interesting producer in New York. Even more astonishing, Joe Papp had accepted to do it.

He did not contact me until after the play had opened. A virile American voice rang to introduce its owner ('This is Joe Papp'). Joe announced that he was as pleased with the production as he was with the reviews. Why didn't I come over and see it? I was starting to tell him where to send the tickets when Joe reminded me that he ran a poor theatre downtown. Bankruptcy stared him daily in the face. The last thing he could afford to do was fly a dramatist over from Europe. I replied that in that case I couldn't afford to come.

A week or two went by before there was another call. This time, Joe, as cheerful as ever, announced he was closing the show. I could hardly have been more surprised. 'But, Joe,' I said – I never did learn that awful showbiz custom of calling him Mr Papp – 'only two weeks ago you were telling me the reviews were excellent.' 'So they are,' said Joe. 'They're terrific. But they're not extractable.' The important thing, Joe explained, was never what a critic said. It was whether you could get a quote out of it. 'If you look at the *New York Times*, it's a good review. But we need something to put on the ads, and the most commercial thing we can find is "David Hare pushes up lilacs out of the deadland."' Joe added, 'Somehow I don't see that line in neon.'

There is, in this early anecdote, so much I came to admire about Joe – his hardy heroism, his mordant humour, his readiness to accept his fate and to move on. For a man who had accomplished so much, he was devoid of interest in the past. No sooner had he done something than he felt it was time to do something else. At a later point, when I knew him much better, I dubbed him the Emperor of Ruritania – I think it was after we'd all had to wait twenty minutes for a preview to begin in one of his theatres, solely because the producer was late. I remember arguing with him afterwards: 'The show isn't for you, Joe. It's for the audience.' One wag printed rebel T-shirts for the staff emblazoned with the message: 'I work in Ruritania.' It was a joke which Joe found only moderately funny. But, in fact, Joe more resembled Mao Zedong. He believed in constant revolution. And like Mao, Joe tended to decorate his changes of direction with speeches of justification, delivered from a reclining chair behind the desk in his spacious office on Lafayette Street, and some of an almost Castro-like length and energy.

If you never met him, you can't imagine how completely Joe Papp dominated a room. Short, lean, with thick dark eyebrows, Byronic brow and an intense air of windswept concentration, he was everyone's idea of a man of action – never lost either for an analysis or for an unlikely way forward. You could never quite rely on being your normal self in his presence. You would find yourself saying stupid things, because you were always aware that, ultimately, you were being seen through his eyes. One famous actress confessed that she realised the source of her own self-consciousness after a mere nine months of knowing him. 'Oh, I see,' she said to herself one day, as if the likeliest explanation had somehow never occurred to her. 'I'm in love with him.'

Being in love with Joe was the easiest way to deal with him. It was, if you like, the line of least resistance. He was, like many dynamic people, set on capturing your affections and, what's more, forever monitoring you for signs of his success. The more you resisted, the more he redoubled his efforts. There was little doubt that in his opinion it was an outrage, an offence against nature, not to adore him. How could you not? For myself, I managed to accumulate a number of reasons, not least his refusal from 1978 onwards to produce my play *Plenty*. From the moment the National Theatre in London had staged this story of an ex-SOE agent who cannot forget the examples of bravery and heroism she has encountered during the war, its natural destination had seemed to be the Public. Or so everyone kept telling me. 'There's only one theatre in New York where this play belongs,' people would say, in a formulation which invariably sent my spirits plunging. It took four years before Joe called me into his office. 'Well, I suppose I'm going to have to do your play. I'm only doing it in the hope it'll stop everyone telling me to do it.'

To be fair, Joe's four-year reluctance to stage my work was the symptom of a larger prejudice and one with which I was in total sympathy. The 1970s, remember, were one of the high points of British playwriting. Any visitor could hop on a plane, and, in between visiting Harrods and Fortnum & Mason, purchase brand-new plays of the first rank by innumerable splendid dramatists including Trevor Griffiths, Tom Stoppard and Harold Pinter. Joe had long resolved to be the only significant New York producer never to resort to importing English hits. At a time when an American audience needed to hear the voices of its unperformed black and Hispanic playwrights, it was, in his eyes, a contemptible dereliction to go cherry-picking abroad for plays which – crucially – would need no creative input from their American producers.

To do a British play at all was, for Joe, a kind of defeat. He practised positive discrimination before the phrase was popular – and at a time when such a strategy needed courage and vision. He was doing *Plenty*, he said, only because it was the kind of epic political work that the American theatre lacked: shame, he added, that it had to come from an Englishman. The bad grace with which he allowed the play into his schedule became a motif of his behaviour throughout its production. After attending the first run-through in which I had, as director, managed to weld my talented company into an English-seeming ensemble, Joe's only comment was to mutter, 'The girl worries me.' Since 'the girl' was the thirty-year-old Kate Nelligan who had already played the role in London to general acclaim, this was a typically Joe-like response. But things got worse at the dress rehearsal when I realised Kate needed one more costume. I asked for an extra coat she could change into to mark a passage of time. An embarrassed wardrobe mistress was waiting for me later. 'I'm sorry, but Joe's ordered a spending stop on this show until he sees whether it's going to work.' When, at the end of the first preview, the audience rose to their feet to acclaim Kate's performance, I was distracted by the producer already sweeping along the aisle to the exit. Beneath the cheers, I heard him snarling in my ear, 'She gets the coat.'

It was once said of my agent Peggy Ramsay that she despised success, but she didn't much like failure either. *Plenty*, in one way, disappointed Joe because there wasn't much for him to do. In all the time I worked with him, I always felt that he was watching a play only in order to prepare for the far more important drama of his own reaction. Joe was that rare thing: a producer with an intellectual life and a social view. He didn't just put on plays. He sought to change things by the plays he put on. Like so many of his ideas, his founding notion of performing Shakespeare free in the park sprang from social idealism. The tepid commercialism of so much of today's not-for-profit theatre would have horrified a man as interested in politics as he was in show business. Yes, you might bump into Robert De Niro or Al Pacino in Joe's office. But more often you would meet Mayor David Dinkins.

A Chorus Line, his most famous hit, was important to Joe for two different reasons. It went uptown and made his theatre famous with people who would otherwise not have heard of it. It was Joe's conviction that the best place for a radical to work was in the mainstream. He had no interest in being overlooked on the fringe. Like William Shawn, whose editorship at the *New Yorker* did so much to discredit the American venture in Vietnam, Joe believed that the best place to change things is from the centre of the culture. But just as important to Joe was the musical's political metaphor. *A Chorus Line* was about America, and the people who wait to be picked out.

Once *Plenty* was launched on its path to Broadway, Joe set about making sure I remained off-balance. I might be getting rich, but there was no question of my being allowed to be comfortable. Planning ahead as always, he instigated a discussion of who might be willing to take over when Kate came to the end of her engagement. He suggested Sigourney Weaver. I said I liked Sigourney Weaver very much, but I had only seen her in lighter fare. I asked him to give me a little time to think. Next day, without warning, Joe called me over to his office, telling me there was somebody he had always wanted me to meet. Sitting on his sofa was a well-known actress, six foot tall and bewildered. 'David, this is Sigourney Weaver. Sigourney, this is David Hare. He doesn't want you in his play. Now David, tell her why.'

To Sigourney Weaver's credit, she still speaks to me. It shows a fine nature. She was humiliated that day, and so was I. Joe, on the other hand, seemed unabashed. He did such things, I believe, because he hated artists to settle. It was as if he had a superstitious fear that some moral damage might be done if things were felt to be going too well. As it happens, I was able to test and prove this theory because the two successes I offered him – *Plenty* and a play about UNESCO, *A Map of the World*, which found a large and enthusiastic audience – were followed by two controversial flops. The first was the world premiere of a sex-change opera called *The Knife*, and the second, the catastrophic ten-day Broadway run of *The Secret Rapture*. Sure enough, the bumpy reception afforded to both these shows bonded us far more closely than seemed possible in the days of our fractious prosperity. Many producers withdraw when you bring them failure. They treat you as if you've given them a virus. With Joe, failure brought you closer.

The Knife was, in a way, the easier of the two to deal with because its shortcomings were so obviously down to me. The composer Nick Bicât had conceived of a sung-through musical, or maybe opera, in which the central character, played by Mandy Patinkin, would make the journey to Morocco, only to discover, as some transsexuals do, that a change of gender does not necessarily bring a solution to all life's problems. In the first act, Mandy played a man. In the second, a woman. When we put together forty-five minutes of music in a rehearsed workshop on a Friday afternoon in the Anspacher Theater, with lyrics by Tim Rose Price, the effect was magical. I turned at the end to find Joe behind me in floods of tears. But in the process of turning our workshop into a fully-fledged production, I managed to destroy what was best in our work. As director and author of the book, I ended up with a hybrid, something half experimental, half conventional. The production made lame and explicit ideas which in the workshop had been beautiful and fragile. Our treatment of transsexuality was at least thirty years ahead of its time, but, carrying the vase on the always perilous journey from workshop to showroom, I dropped it.

Joe had taken on *The Knife* knowing how ambitious and far-seeing it was. He also knew it was likely to get creamed. He loved musicals. I hated them. But both of us felt that someone had to shake the form up. (This was in 1987, way before *Jerry Springer: The Opera* and *Caroline, or Change*.) Joe told me he had been approached at an early preview by the veteran composer Jules Stein, who had asked, 'You're planning to take this to Broadway? Well, my advice is take it one act at a time. Do the first act this season, and keep the second act for next season, because that's all Broadway can manage.' Stein had added, 'I don't know if I like it, but, boy, I'm glad somebody's done it.' Predictably, through all my agony of self-doubt, Joe had remained strong and resolute, rising to the occasion, sitting beside me through 29 previews, offering good advice. We barely quarrelled at all.

After the first night, he called me to his office. A lot of people had adored the evening, but to adore it, you had to be on its side. If you let it touch you, it would. At the time, the *New York Times* critic was Frank Rich, who was viscerally opposed not only to Joe's regime, but to anything he smelt was edgy or risk-taking. He was the classic aristocrat who hates it when the staff get above themselves. Joe read out Rich's excoriating review, giving passionate emphasis to every dismissive phrase and lousy adjective. At the end of the reading, Joe put the paper down, knowing he had just lost a million dollars. 'Now that', he said, 'is what I call a bad review.' He turned and looked at me. 'So, David, what do you want to do in my theatre next?'

It would be fair to say that at that moment, in all its stagy glory, I moved onto a different plane with Joe. I had already, by that time, dimly begun to perceive that the only thing that matters is loyalty. Now I knew. Without it, we're all just a bunch of idiots. Nothing moves me more in my chosen art form than the belief that there is something more important than the particular piece of work on which we are engaged at the time. Joe understood this better than anyone. Thanks to the depth of his politics, it didn't mean much to Joe whether a single show went well or badly. What mattered was the ongoing story of what the Public represented – a continually innovating theatre connected to the ethnically diverse society it mirrored. By those standards, with its sexual radicalism and its attempt to blow fresh air into the ailing form of the stage musical, *The Knife* was a contribution – whether it worked for the whole audience or not.

It would be too much to say that Joe received the closing of our last venture together with the same equanimity. On the contrary. For the only time in my life I saw my producer defeated. From the moment he read my play about Thatcherism, *The Secret Rapture*, Joe had resolved to attack afresh the recurring problem of how you produce a serious drama in New York. He had watched too many plays fall into the gap between the talented and the viable for him not to want to conceive some entirely new way of presenting them. The solution, he decided, was to run *The Secret Rapture* off-Broadway in his own 300-seat theatre for as long as we needed to get it right, and not move it to Broadway until we were ready. We would then let the critics have their crack at it. The plan, in other words, was to use Lafayette Street the way other producers used out-of-town.

We had been running happily in the Newman Theater for three weeks to full houses when a senior editor at the *New York Times* called Joe up and accused him of making a monkey of his paper. He told Joe that the *Times* would not permit a play by a known author to continue unreviewed. Either Joe was to speed us at once to Broadway, or else their critic would walk in uninvited and buy a ticket. The editor decorated this threat with a lot of pious garbage about the public's right to know, but neither Joe nor the editor mistook what was really at stake: power. The *Times* was not willing to yield an inch of its influence over the New York theatre. The brilliant maverick producer was being called to heel.

In the face of the *Times*, Joe backed down and moved us to Broadway at once. We walked straight into the mantrap the newspaper had set for us. When their critic delivered his predictable review, aimed at reinforcing the newspaper's writ, Joe tried to kick up a storm. Without asking me, he released to *Variety* the text of a private letter I had sent to Frank Rich, and instituted a series of hopeless meetings with the Shubert Organization to discuss whether we could arrange a boycott of the *Times* and persuade the entire theatre community to move all their expensive advertising to *Newsday*. But you could tell Joe's heart wasn't in it. Nor was mine. Unknown to me, Joe's occasional absences from my side in these difficult weeks were caused by the first of his trips to Boston for treatment of the cancer which would eventually kill him. I flew back from my father's funeral in England for the play's grim wake. Joe sat beside me on a banquette in a small restaurant. 'If they won't let me do this play, they won't let me do anything.'

Over the next two years we were able to talk some more, both in person and on the phone, as Joe's health declined. There was a sweetness, both in him and in the feeling between us, which had not been there before. We both took the closing of *The Secret Rapture* very hard indeed, but Joe turned his attention to ensuring the continuity of his beloved theatre and of developing his new passion for watching and studying birds. One night, in October 1991, after a delirious day with my future wife, whom I'd met 48 hours earlier, I returned home to find the light blinking '26' on my answering machine. Every single message was from a different person. Nearly all began, 'I felt you ought to know' or 'You've probably heard'. In fact, I hadn't heard anything because, at the very moment my new life was beginning, Joe's had ended.

The next day Caryl Churchill called. 'David, everyone who believed in us is dead.'

How do I sum up what Joe meant to me? I never met anyone in whom radicalism and showmanship were in such fruitful collision. He created the model of a European subsidised theatre – six houses, God knows how many plays – in a capitalist culture. Who else would dream of selling telephone tickets by having customers dial the letters J-O-E-P-A-P-P to reach the box office? Who else would design a logo for his theatre with the face of Shakespeare looking remarkably like Joe Papp? He did more than anyone in American theatre history to advance the cause of minority writers, directors and actors. There were times when his wrong-footing and perversity could drive you crazy. There were also times when his preference for his personal vision over the common wisdom was glorious. When I look back at how he behaved towards one playwright and one playwright's work – prickly in success, valiant, loyal, and stalwart in failure – I understand one thing. Joe Papp was never happier, never stronger than when you needed him.

(2006)

YOUNG CHEKHOV: THE BIRTH
OF THE NEW

I had first adapted Ivanov *for Ralph Fiennes to perform at the Almeida Theatre in 1997. From the moment Jonathan Kent and Ian McDiarmid suggested I move on to* Platonov, *I dreamed of a day when all three of Chekhov's young plays could be presented together. This dream was realised at the Chichester Festival Theatre in 2015.*

In a deliberately provocative essay, the critic James Wood compares Chekhov with Ibsen, and, as critics will, finds in Chekhov's favour. Ibsen, Wood believes, orders life into three trim acts. The Norwegian thinks of his characters as envoys, sent into the world in order to convey the dramatic ironies and ideas of their author. The people in the Russian plays, by contrast, 'act like free consciousness, not as owned literary characters'. Wood rates Chekhov next to Shakespeare because these two alone, among the world's great writers, respect the absolute complexity of life, never allowing their creations to be used for any other purpose than being themselves. The special genius of the human beings you meet in Chekhov's plays and short stories is that they don't have to behave like people in a purposeful drama. 'Chekhov's characters', Wood declares, 'forget to be Chekhov's characters.'

Who can deny that this is an alluring and obviously potent idea? Who doesn't love the notion that there once existed an author so free that he was able to summon up men and women who trail a sense of mystery as profound as human beings do in real life? Of course, it would be wonderful if plays and books could be written which were seen not to reorder life, but which we were able to experience as if they were life itself. What a marvellous thing that would be! But behind Wood's apparently novel theory – boiled down: let's all applaud a writer who is not felt to intervene – you can hear the echo of another critical battle which has been raging for over a hundred years since Chekhov's death. Wood is firing a fresh round of artillery on behalf of that section of the playwright's admirers who value him as the ultimate universalist, the man too squeamish to say anything too specific about his own time and his own class. They think of their hero as a portraitist. But Wood ignores that other, equally vociferous section of admirers who prefer to believe that their man was as political, as social and as specific a writer as Gorky or Tolstoy. They think of him as a moralist.

It is my own conviction that we can't address these contentious questions unless we take time to consider those plays which Chekhov wrote, as it were, before he was Chekhov. *The Cherry Orchard*, *The Three Sisters* and *Uncle Vanya* have been in the international repertory ever since they were written, sometimes giving more pleasure to actors who relish their ensemble qualities than to audiences who, in second-rate productions, find them listless. But less attention is paid to the playwright's earlier work. It is essential to see these vibrant and much more direct plays for what they are – thrilling sunbursts of youthful anger and romanticism – rather than for what they portend.

There is no duller and less fruitful way of looking at the key works of Chekhov's theatrical beginnings than merely as maquettes for the later plays. Certainly, we can all amuse ourselves by drawing up lists of characters and plot incidents in *Platonov* which recur in *The Cherry Orchard* and *Uncle Vanya*. But as we tick off these motifs – the failed suicides, the mismatched lovers, the sales of the estates – the danger is that we ignore equally powerful material and themes whose special interest is that they never occur again.

No, *Platonov* does not have the intricate, superbly wrought surface of *The Three Sisters*. Who could claim that so many hours of sometimes repetitive and overwritten speechifying exhibit the faultless literary control for which Chekhov later became known? But *Platonov* does have, in its very wildness, a sort of feverish ambition, a desire, almost, to put the whole of Russia on the stage, while at the same time focusing comically on one of its most sophisticated victims. Where is the parallel for this, not just in Chekhov's work, but in anyone else's?

The text of *Platonov* is so prolix that the most successful adaptations have, significantly, tended to be the freest. When Michael Frayn wrote his popular comedy *Wild Honey* for the National Theatre in 1984, he admitted that he treated the text 'as if it were the rough draft of one of my own plays'. When Nikita Mikhalkov made his 1985 film *An Unfinished Piece for Mechanical Piano*, he reallocated lines, banished half the characters, abandoned the substantive plot, and shoehorned in ideas and images of his own. But my strategy, both more and less radical than that of my two gifted predecessors, was that I should try to stick, in architecture at least, to Chekhov's original plan. I would clear away massive amounts of repetition and indulgence, I would recoin and rebalance much of the dialogue, I would hack through acres of brushwood, but nevertheless I would aim that the audience should see the play in something recognisable as the form in which Chekhov left it.

It was a risky undertaking. *Platonov* may seem an odd-shaped play. It can seem like a man who sets off for a walk in one direction, but who is lured by the beauty of the landscape towards another destination entirely. The first act, sometimes entirely cut in early English-language productions, has a gorgeous breadth and sweep which leads you to expect an evening in the company of a whole community. The second centres on a long, almost *Godot*-like meditation between two lost souls. By the time the third is under way, you are witnessing a series of painful and funny duologues, all with Platonov himself as the common partner, and by the fourth, you are, with a bit of luck, adjusting yourself to a climax of feverish hysteria. No wonder commentators dismissed this ambitious story of steam trains and lynchings for 'uncertainty of tone'. A faithful performance of *Platonov* will test to the limit the idea that an evening in a playhouse needs to be held together in one governing style.

Even in my compressed version, enemies of the play will call it a ragbag. Let them. For me, something wholly original lies at its spine. The form, often accused of being undisciplined, can more truly be seen as a kind of narrowing, a deliberate irising down onto one particular character. Chekhov sets off to give us a broad-brush view of a society which is rotten with money, drink and hypocrisy. Capitalism is just arriving, and its practices, all too recognisable today, are sweeping aside a privileged class which no longer knows how to maintain its way of life. Ruling-class attitudes have survived long after ruling-class influence has gone. But then, once he has established the context of his vision, Chekhov goes on to embody the contradictions of this superfluous class in one single individual.

The schoolteacher Platonov has squandered his inherited fortune. Again, critics usually portray him as a small-town Lothario, seeking bored amusement in the pursuit of women. But if we examine what Chekhov actually wrote, we will find a hero who is, in fact, surprisingly reluctant to consummate his relationship with at least one of the women who are in love with him. Far from being a determined seducer, 'the most interesting man in the region' is, on the contrary, a person to whom things happen – sometimes at his wish, sometimes by accident. In his relationships, he tries not for easy conquest, but rather to discover in love a purpose and meaning which elude him elsewhere. The tired, traditional notion of the provincial Don Juan suddenly breathes with humanity and contradiction.

It is hard not to see a wry autobiographical element in the twenty-year-old author's appraisal of a man whose main problem in life is that women find him irresistible. But no such identification can explain the confidence with which the women themselves are drawn. In the figure of the general's widow, Anna Petrovna, first played unforgettably by Helen McCrory, and then later by Nina Sosanya, Chekhov creates one of the great heroines of the Russian stage – an educated, intelligent and loving woman who can find no place in the world for her love, her intelligence or her education. In the compassion Chekhov extends both to Sasha, Platonov's religiously devout wife, and to Sofya, the idealistic young woman who is set on fire by Platonov's too-easy radical rhetoric, we find a degree of imaginative sympathy which would be remarkable in a writer twice or three times Chekhov's age.

In short, then, we have a great example of Chekhov exposed – not, as in later plays, seeking to hide his personality under the cover of his creations, but more, like Osborne through Jimmy Porter, willing to let his own passion and his own political despair spill onto the stage. This writer is not at all James Wood's stringless puppet-master, but rather a man unafraid by a mix of direct address, monologue, farce and tragedy to let us know how strongly he feels about the social decay around him. Perhaps because Rex Harrison played the part at the Royal Court in 1960 when he was almost twice the age the author specifies – he says twenty-seven, Harrison was fifty-two – there is an expectation in Britain of Platonov being played, when the role is played at all, by an actor who is far too old. But this play, above all plays, is a terrible tragedy of youth. Young Chekhov is hotter than old.

*

I've tried to be original. I have not introduced a single villain or a single angel (though I haven't been able to abstain from fools); nor have I accused or vindicated anyone. Whether or not I've succeeded I can't tell. Korsh and the actors are sure the play will work. I'm not so sure. The actors don't understand it and say the most ridiculous things, they're badly miscast, I'm constantly at war with them. Had I known I'd never have got involved with it.

Chekhov's own words about his first performed play *Ivanov* chime with Maxim Gorky's observation: 'How lonely Chekhov is. How little he's understood.' With hindsight we know that Chekhov was about to begin the process of banishing melodrama from the nineteenth-century stage, but as a result it has been easy and convenient to forget the fact that he once wrote an exceptionally good melodrama himself. Because he tended to disparage the play in his private correspondence, and because its early performances were so disastrous, the author implicitly gave permission to anyone who wanted to label it as clumsy. Originally drafted in only two weeks, the play uses monologue and direct address. It features a hero who makes long speeches. It satirises a certain layer of society in much broader strokes than those Chekhov later favoured. But what entitles us to think these techniques are not deliberate, and in their way just as skilfully deployed as the more muted strategies the author later adopted? Unless we can admit that *Ivanov* is not a lesser play, but simply different from his later work, we will miss its significance.

Nothing has been more damaging to our feeling for Chekhov's plays than the way his admirers have tended to represent the author himself. I have often had to explain to enraptured young women that the object of their love is dead, and has been for a good long time now. Encouraged by suitably enigmatic photographs, we have tolerated the idea that the dramatist was some sort of all-purpose secular saint, living six feet above the rest of the human race, able to observe mankind's foibles with a medical man's detached and witty irony. Anyone who has bothered to establish the facts of his life would know how far off the mark this notion is.

The real Chekhov is complex, testy and troubled. Indeed, to that tiresome school of academics who believe that literary criticism consists of marking off a writer's every line against a contemporary checklist of fashionable 'errors', the saintly Chekhov comes through with his halo looking distinctly askew.

When we hear this supposedly virtuous playwright saying that when he entered a room full of good-looking women, he 'melted like a Yid contemplating his ducats' we may begin to suspect that our man is not quite who he is commonly made out to be. When he elsewhere observes that the most complimentary thing you can say about a woman is that 'she doesn't think like a woman'; when we discover him in Monte Carlo, fretfully revising an infallible system and then losing 500 francs in two days; when we catch him referring to his one-time Jewish girlfriend as 'Efros the Nose'; when we find him in Sri Lanka 'glutting himself on dusky women', we are already waving a vigorous goodbye to the floppy-hatted and languorous stereotype.

A singular virtue of the play *Ivanov* is that it gives us a clear sight of this more robust Chekhov, and one who is happy to use some quite orthodox dramatic conventions – each act climaxes with what he calls 'a punch on the nose' – to tackle contemporary themes. Here is a full-blooded writer, willing to address the ugliness of Russian anti-Semitism head on, and dramatising a conflict from within himself in a way that is both deeply felt and funny. For once, his own feelings and thoughts are plainly on show.

It could hardly be otherwise. The dominating theme of *Ivanov* is honesty. It would have been impossible for Chekhov to have written a play which asks what real honesty is, and – just as important – what its price is, without allowing access to his own personality. Although the play, like his later work, may be said to weave together a whole variety of threads, nothing is more striking in it than the deliberate contrast between the self-confident Doctor Lvov and the more cautious Ivanov. The play's defining argument is between a young doctor who thinks that honesty is to do with blurting out offensive truths, and the central character who insists with a wisdom which is pre-Freudian that no one can achieve honesty unless they have the self-knowledge to examine their own motives.

In this debate there is no doubt with whom Chekhov's sympathies lie. 'If my Ivanov comes across as a blackguard or superfluous man, and the doctor as a great man, if no one understands why Anna and Sasha love Ivanov, then my play has evidently failed and there can be no question of having it produced.' But for all his protestations of partiality, Chekhov makes sure to provide Ivanov with an opponent who is, in an odd way, as compelling as the hero, and sometimes almost his shadow. Chekhov leaves us to work out for ourselves whether honesty resides in judging others or in refusing to judge them.

Apart from the charge of technical immaturity, the play has also had to survive the impression that, in Ivanov himself, it presents a hero who is excessively, even morbidly self-pitying. Yet in saying this, critics ignore Chekhov's stated intention to kill off once and for all the strain of self-indulgent melancholy which he believed disfigured Russian literature. 'I have long cherished the audacious notion of summing up all that has hitherto been written about complaining and melancholy people, and would have my Ivanov proclaim the ultimate in such writing.' Far

179

from idealising the so-called superfluous man, Chekhov seeks to send him packing. It was Ralph Fiennes who, at the Almeida in 1997, in a moment of revelation for the British theatre, finally played the part the way the author wanted, revealing Ivanov not as a landowner lost in useless introspection, but rather a man who found the whole Russian tradition of introspection and self-pity humiliating. As Fiennes portrayed him, Ivanov was not a stereotype. He was a man fighting with all his willpower not to surrender to a stereotype. He was determined to refuse the comfort of falsely dramatising his feelings. Viewed in this light, the play's tragic ending, which provided the author with so much difficulty, seemed to have a terrible logic.

Ivanov is a play with which Chekhov, for all his rewriting, never felt satisfied. Yet as so often there are ways in which early literary struggle provides an infinitely richer experience than many works which we like to claim as mature.

*

Of all nineteenth-century plays *The Seagull* is most insistently modern. It is also the most adapted. I would not have dared to add to what is already a long list of successful adaptations unless I had wanted to tie these three plays together into a single experience, and to present the final play in an illuminating context. Because *The Seagull* deals with an artistic argument between the avant-garde and the traditional, it updates peculiarly well. Anya Reiss's recent transposition of the play to the Isle of Man in the present day – people go into town in Land Rovers, not on horseback – seemed to have none of the usual problems of doing what Jonathan Miller called 'schlepping a play up the motorway'. On the contrary, it was triumphantly apt and alive. Those reviewers who complained of the presence of fridges, sunglasses and high heels in Luc Bondy's stunning production for the Vienna Burgtheater seemed blind to the beauty of what the director was doing: just nudging a play which is set on the cusp of change into a visual language which made it fresher and more immediate.

Presented, as on this occasion, as the climax to his work as a young man, you may notice what is hardly apparent in a stand-alone production. The bones of the plot are pretty routine. A promising young woman is ruined by an older man, and cast aside. Her dreams and those of her despairing boyfriend are brutally destroyed. We are, if you care to notice, once more in the realm of melodrama, as we were in *Platonov* and in *Ivanov*. For the third time, there will be a death in the final moments of the play. But now, in this climactic work, something new has arrived, which is not purely a matter of technique. Chekhov has found a sophisticated way of burying meaning deep in texture, of leaving as much unsaid as said. But also, instead of giving us single characters striving for individual self-expression, he has found a marvellous ability to suggest something beyond them, something inexpressible. His characters are starting to be victims of events and changes in themselves which it is almost impossible for them to recognise or understand. He is putting them under the eye of eternity.

Anyone who wants to obey the implications of Chekhov calling his play a comedy will find plenty of material in the characters' self-ignorance. At one level, Arkadina can't accept her career is on the slide; however much he discourses on the subject, Trigorin can't accept he's second-rate; and Konstantin can't accept that he can't write. But, at another level, these truths are partial, speaking as much to the characters' fears as they do to the reality. And as the play deepens, easy judgements become hard. Is Nina a good actress or is she not? Is Arkadina a terrible mother, or is she not dealing with a son whose downward path is predestined and whom nobody can save from himself? Masha's decision to abandon all her romantic hopes and longings may seem expensive. But did she ever, at any point, have any real choice?

It is the unknowability of fate which pulls this play towards greatness. The balance in writing here has changed, but there is enough of Chekhov's early romanticism still showing to make it the most perfect, and most perfectly achieved, play he ever wrote. Are the characters victims of their traits, or are they choosing paths which might have led elsewhere? In *Platonov*, time is something which stretches ahead, meaningless. In *Ivanov*, it represents waste, like an abacus of failure. But in *The Seagull*, with its clever structure of inter-act jumps, time represents something more powerful: both the element in which we act out our own misfortunes, but also the reason for so many of them. This is a play about young people. Even Arkadina is only forty-three. But the whole set of characters seems to be struggling against some terrible force which strips them and robs them, however they behave. Angry at having to explain to a young woman how punishing his profession is, Trigorin launches into an affair for no other reason than because he can. Yes, of course, it has a terrible effect on Nina, its victim. But it also leaves Trigorin sadder, diminished, a husk.

The Seagull was famously a play made by a great second production. On its first outing, in an indifferent production, it flopped. This seems to me no coincidence. With *The Seagull*, Chekhov is for the first time beginning to write plays which crucially depend on how you do them. At the outset, as a short-story writer, he condescended to the form of theatre, vowing each time never to go anywhere near a theatre again. But by the time he writes *The Seagull*, you can feel his increasing fascination with the form, and a new desire to advance the history of that form. He begins, in short, to take theatre seriously.

On the surface, *The Seagull* is a play about theatre, and most certainly about art. For that reason, perhaps it has a history of encouraging exceptional performances. It is a play in which actors as diverse as James Mason, Penelope Wilton, Vanessa Redgrave, George Devine and Carey Mulligan have all done among their greatest work. But the struggle to create something lasting and worthwhile in life is what drives the play. Theatre is only the metaphor. Chekhov's own youth is ending and it is ending with a new determination not to knock away the past but to try, in however doomed a fashion, to find his way to some sort of future. It is a very long distance in this trilogy of plays from the character of the criminal Osip in *Platonov*, who lives in the forest like a medieval thief, to the young Konstantin, dreaming of an art which has never been seen before. As we watch, or as we read, we are moving from the nineteenth century to the twentieth, and, implicitly to our own. We are seeing the birth of the new.

(2015)

UNCLE VANYA: NEVER THE
SAME TWICE

Rupert Everett persuaded me in 2019 to adapt one of Chekhov's mature plays, in spite of my feeling that Louis Malle's film could not be bettered. But Uncle Vanya *gripped and fascinated me as I got to know it.*

Uncle Vanya has always been the most elusive of all Chekhov's plays. It's never the same twice. As with certain mysterious films like *Citizen Kane*, however often you see them, it is difficult to hold in your mind the order of scenes and events. Whenever you go back, you're surprised. When I first saw Michael Redgrave playing Vanya in Laurence Olivier's production at the Chichester Festival Theatre in 1962, the play itself seemed romantic but seamless. By the time Paul Scofield played the role at the Royal Court in 1970, the tone, in Christopher Hampton's version, had become far sharper and crueller. When Wallace Shawn appeared in Louis Malle's film, *Vanya on 42nd Street*, in 1994, the extremes of feeling were rendered feverish through the luscious intimacy of the camerawork. Whole swathes of the play, faithfully translated but freshly acted, emerged unrecognisable. And Paul Rhys, in Robert Icke's Almeida version in 2016, took the central character as near to the madhouse as he's ever been.

It's not just that *Vanya* soaks up a bewildering variety of interpretation. (All the above evenings were, by the way, first-rate. Unlike *The Cherry Orchard*, *Uncle Vanya* generates great productions.) It's also that, in the theatre, it's often hard to discern exactly what it's about. The subtitle 'Scenes from Country Life' tells us Chekhov is suggesting, at the most satirical level, that the Russian countryside is very far from being the idealised place of art and literature. The land itself is being poisoned and ripped up to no good purpose, and the alternation of extreme seasonal heat and cold can be well-nigh unbearable if you have to live there. But critics who go on to suggest that the play is a tragedy of middle age – about that moment when we are all forced to realise that we have not achieved what we wanted – are making a point as uninteresting as those who write of *King Lear* as if it were a medical drama of senility. It may describe the play, but it doesn't illuminate it.

My own approach to making an English-language version of *Uncle Vanya* has been via my involvement with adapting Chekhov's younger work. In a season, first at Chichester in 2015, then at the National Theatre the following year, Jonathan Kent directed *Platonov*, *Ivanov* and *The Seagull* so that audiences could see all three in a single day. The first two plays, sometimes sprawling, sometimes unfocused, needed a certain amount of dramaturgical rearrangement, even if the third one was famously perfect. But however discreet my interventions, I wanted to put the three plays together to make the point that Chekhov had usually been admired as a cool writer, perfecting the technique of hiding behind the trelliswork of his characters and lending his own voice to none. However, as a young man, in his furious, desperate heroes Platonov and Ivanov, he had manifested as a very hot writer indeed. The author's own anger is the fuel for three turbocharged plays.

Something of that heat, I hope, has come through in the way I've chosen to frame the present play. Chekhov never saw Stanislavsky's Moscow Arts production, and admittedly he was horrified to hear of the final scene between Elena and Astrov being so over-directed that the doctor came across 'as a drowning man clutching at straws'. But that particular reservation doesn't mean that the play elsewhere is not, sometimes comically, full of passion, rage and strong feeling.

The play's story can be simply summarised. Into an ordered and regular household come two new inhabitants, an irritable professor and his young wife, who, in the space of a few months, cause chaos, one by their selfishness, and the other by their sexual allure. Between them, they manage, in the time between their arrival and their departure, to have most of the household questioning their purpose in life, their happiness and, at times, their sanity.

What troubles most people in the play is the question of what they should do. The theme is symphonically stated very early on when Vanya admits to the fact that he now does nothing. Vanya has worked on the estate for many years, facilitating and admiring the intellectual theories of his brother-in-law Professor Serebryakov, and going along with his mother's obsessive scrutiny of political pamphlets. But, for reasons only hinted at, Vanya has, during the previous year, become violently disillusioned, unable to believe that the life of the mind has much use or connection in the world at large. He no longer dreams of the realisation of ideas. His only speech of possible fulfilment is when he imagines taking the woman he is in love with into his arms and sheltering her from the storm outside. At other times he is gripped with a fury about his own uselessness and waste which borders on the pathological.

In contrast, the person who does spend his life doing things – at least until this fated summer – is the doctor, Astrov. But, as Sonya realises, it is almost impossible for anyone to deal on a daily basis with the real problems of Russia without becoming coarsened and cynical at the scale of the task. At a time when life expectancy in France was forty-seven, in Russia it was still only thirty-one for men, and thirty-three for women. Half of the children born in the late nineteenth century were dying before the age of five. The insanitary conditions in which peasants lived meant they were prey to cholera, typhus, dysentery, worms, syphilis, diphtheria and malaria. No wonder the professor's wife, Yelena – on the page, far more intelligent and acute than in some misleading stage portrayals – reacts in disbelief to the idea of going out and helping. Only in literary novels, she says, do people go and minister to the poor.

Astrov starts the play alcoholic, and haunted by the memory of a recent patient who has died on the operating table under anaesthetic, possibly when Astrov was drunk. Both he and Vanya appear traumatised, one by a real death and the other by a death of belief. Astrov is therefore throwing himself with even more determination into rewilding. He sees human beings as in danger of consuming their own future. The most practical thing anyone can do in response to the devastation of the environment is to ensure that, even if this generation cannot be happy on a planet they are forced through their own ignorance and need to destroy, nevertheless they can serve, by creative replanting, to ensure the happiness of future, more enlightened generations.

It is this contrast between an intellectual class which looks only to its own ideas, and a larger Russia which is mired in squalor and disease, which gives the play its special bite. It goes without saying that it is this contrast – a contrast of extreme inequality – which also makes the drama distinctively modern. Chekhov admired people who do, and mistrusted people who just talk. One of his most important works is the report he wrote when he went to Siberia to expose the full horror of prison conditions there. Clearly, in his fiction, Chekhov never tells you what he would like you to believe. He wrote to a psychologist friend, 'A psychologist should not pretend to understand what he does not understand. Nor should he convey that impression. We shall not play the charlatan, and we shall declare frankly that nothing is clear in this world. Only fools and charlatans know and understand everything.' But this characteristic refusal to tell audiences what they should think does not include any reluctance to tell them what they should be thinking about.

Look at your own life, he's saying. What use is it? And what can you do?

(2019)

MERE FACT, MERE FICTION

A lecture delivered at the Royal Society of Literature on 12 April 2010

Last week I celebrated a melancholy anniversary. It was forty years to the day since the premiere of my first full-length play at the Hampstead Theatre Club on 6 April 1970. Anyone old enough to remember will know that the prefabricated building was moved first from one side of the Swiss Cottage car park to the other – and then back again to somewhere nearer its original location, but now in sturdier premises. Somewhere in transit the word 'Club' dropped from the shingle. In other words, in four decades, theatre culture has changed, if not out of all recognition, at least significantly.

One further example. If you set to writing plays in the post-war years, it was necessary, or at least expected, to pass through a portal of approval. In prospect, this gave a comfortable, orderly feeling to the idea of being a British dramatist. Kenneth Tynan, a humanist dandy, guarded the portal on one side from his influential position as the *Observer*'s drama critic. Harold Hobson, a Conservative Francophile whose life had been changed at the age of ten by the sight of a Bible in the illuminated window of a Christian Science church, guarded the other side from the *Sunday Times*. A novice playwright had every reason to expect that a life in the theatre would involve attracting and then retaining the interest, if not of these particular men, at least of whoever took their place.

Harold Hobson's name was linked with Beckett's and with Pinter's. Tynan's fortunes rose with his impassioned advocacy of the work of John Osborne. These were the writers they championed and whose view of the world fired them up. They were interlinked because of a profound correspondence of belief. Today, no such correspondence exists. No living theatrical figure is linked with any particular critic. Kenneth Tynan, eighty-three years old last week had he not been taken by emphysema, would be devastated to know that to work in the British theatre it is no longer necessary even to know the name of the *Observer*'s theatre reviewer, let alone to read them.

Most people have an understandable nostalgia for what felt like a common culture, even if, over the years, bitter experience left few practitioners with much trust in those delegated to be its guardians. If deference has disappeared from many areas of British life, surely it is because many of its beneficiaries were found out to be undeserving. The growth of diversity both in the theatre audience and in the places it sharpens its opinions has brought only benefit to any dramatist whose first love is for experiment and innovation. And newspapers which once enjoyed such power find themselves discovering what it is like to live with the threat of working in a minority form.

Throughout the 1980s and beyond, militant propaganda for the free market aimed to reach out into many spheres beyond the economic. The aims of the revolution were cultural as much as political. Norman Tebbit was once asked why the Thatcherism in which he had played such an important part had created a society he so disliked. If liberating private enterprise from the shackles of the state had indeed been such an invigorating success, why were the consequences of that success so repellent to him? Lord Tebbit replied that Conservative governments of his generation had taken on such a massive task in fixing the economy that they had had no time to fix the culture.

He was being too modest. In those days, there was no shortage of fellow-travellers happy to direct their fire against the most communal of art forms. For years no Murdoch paper let a week go by without some loyal employee railing against their own definition of elitism – elitism being best represented by the state-subsidised British theatre. Why, conservative commentators asked week after week, were the routines of theatre-going so tedious? Why were the audiences so smug? Why were only a few hundred people admitted to the auditorium each night? Why were a further 5,000 million excluded? Why, most of all, did plays continue to address moral and political questions which belonged more properly to the nineteenth century, and which had been definitively answered by the resurgence of an invigorated capitalism? Wasn't the form itself exhausted? Wasn't cinema hipper?

Today, such attitudes themselves look dated. Having so long prophesied The Death of the Theatre, the prophets have woken to find themselves writhing in the coils of a problem rather closer to home called The Death of the Newspaper. What a reversal of fortune! Who could have foreseen it? Research tells us that a new generation of young people from all over the country is once more choosing to go to the theatre. They seem to value its oddness, its quality of difference. Far from fearing an opportunity to concentrate, the young relish it. Whereas they appear a lot less certain about needing to match their impressions of the world against opinionated sheets of paper.

If the free market is indeed the moral courtroom which its admirers claim, what a judgement is being visited on Fleet Street. What a pack of failures the editors must be! No artistic director of a theatre could survive such a plummeting loss of income and popularity without being sacked by their board. Surely it must be, according to those iron laws of the market which newspapers have done so much to propagate, that consumers are today buying fewer newspapers because those newspapers are poor products? The people writing for them must be no good at writing. QED. Or will journalists henceforth be humbled by the decline of their own industry into less readily assuming that whatever is most popular must necessarily be most worthwhile?

The obvious absurdity of this proposition, and its roots in that same false logic which has had such currency throughout the Blair–Thatcher ascendancy, should not divert us from subtler, more interesting questions about the relationship between art and journalism, between fact and fiction. It is several of these which I aim to address tonight.

When asked to name the best British film of the last twenty-five years, without thinking I nominated Adam Curtis's documentary series *The Power of Nightmares*, which examines how politicians have exploited the so-called war on terror in order to transform themselves from managers to saviours of their nation. My mind went straight to a BBC documentary rather than anything seen at my local Odeon, because, clearly, *The Power of Nightmares* seemed more ambitious than most better-known fictional work. If we give Curtis's film a full-body scan, the diagnosis would be that it passes some of the most traditional – if controversial – tests of art. For a start, nobody could miss the fact that it had been created by one exceptional imagination. Behind its images lay some rich associative thinking. It advanced a way of considering Western leaders which made you see familiar figures in a new light. But if you also investigated its technique, its use of what you might call scrap footage – from advertising, from feature films, from training films, as well as from more usual documentary sources – it not only adopted the methods of some of the twentieth century's most important visual artists, it also attained some of their same haunting strangeness.

I have always believed that works of art depend on metaphor. They must be about more than themselves. An Andrew Marr television series about British history in the first half of the twentieth century is full of interesting anecdotes, one anecdote after another – here's an evacuated village, here are some servicemen dancing, here are three famous men at Yalta. But because these anecdotes do not add up to a story that suggests other stories, because they do not throw light on anything apart from their immediate subject, and because the images the ideas generate are pretty banal – Marr walking by the sea, Marr walking across fields, Marr in a busy street – the viewer would conclude that whatever he or she is watching, it is not art. Marr may be a great teacher, he is certainly a very good journalist, an accomplished tour guide to what has happened and to what is known, but, by my personal definition, the one thing he cannot be, at least on television, is an artist.

In one provocative statement, Waldemar Januszczak, then Head of Arts Programming at Channel 4, expressed his own complex self-hatred. He proposed that there was no need any more to make television programmes about artists because, he argued, a television programme was itself a work of art. Television had spent too long in the position of a waiter, bringing art in to the viewer on a silver salver. In the modern world, he said, television had no good reason to continue feeling subservient. Fawning profiles of artists were old hat. Television did not have to illuminate Bacon. It was Bacon.

Of course, such economically convenient reasoning at once blew wind-assisted through the offices of the channel controllers. Words cannot convey how delighted they were with this cute piece of postmodernism. What a rare pleasure to be let off an expensive hook by one of their own! If any idiot with a camera sounding off about anything they fancied was art, it gave the bosses, with results we all know, a reputable excuse to drop formal arts programming more or less altogether from their majority channels. Television, it was said, existed to be art, not to bring news of it. Strange this, because Ken Russell did not seem in the least subservient when he made his films about Delius and about Elgar. Russell seemed all too happy to accept these composers as masters, and then, in his turn, to demonstrate what their mastery had released in him. Namely, mastery.

The example of Russell making such brilliant television out of brilliant music might, you think, once and for all dispatch certain questions of category. But there is still plenty of dismaying evidence to prove how conjoined art and snobbery will always be. Over forty years ago Philip Roth put his finger on a problem which, in the following years, was going to challenge the novelist's profession as much as mine. He wrote that 'The actuality is continually outdoing our talents, and the culture tosses up figures daily that are the envy of any novelist.' It would be an unusual artist who did not feel that this difficulty had deepened in the new century. Having glibly argued for so many years that artists might do better looking to the world around them than always to the minutiae of their own feelings, even I have been taken aback by the sheer abundance of subject matter available in recent times. I remember saying that it was always valuable for a writer to go out and be rebuked by reality. But recently we have not been so much rebuked as overwhelmed. A working dramatist, I have found myself finishing plays about the privatisation of the railways, about the diplomatic process leading up to the invasion of Iraq, about the corruption of Labour Party funding, about Foreign Office complicity in torture and, most recently, about the financial crisis precipitated by the behaviour of the banks. But this kind of timely writing which seeks, as Balzac's work once did, to provide society with its secretarial record, continues to attract reproach from those good souls who believe that the results cannot be regarded as 'proper' plays – in the sense, say, that Sophocles or Jean Racine write 'properly'.

Particular objection – usually inarticulate – is made to the use of other people's dialogue. No sooner had a genre called verbatim drama been identified and given its lowering title than sceptics appeared arguing that it was unacceptable to copy dialogue down, rather than to make it up. People who did this, they said, were called journalists, not artists. But anyone who gives verbatim theatre a moment's thought – or rather, a dog's chance – will conclude that the matter is not as simple as it first looks. Nor are its moral implications.

In the autumn of 2006, I was working in New York. My luck was that I could therefore go to the Lincoln Center Theater to see Jack O'Brien's superb production of Tom Stoppard's trilogy of plays, *The Coast of Utopia*. After the first evening, we were set fair. Here was the kind of epic work which wove the lives and ideas of individual nineteenth-century Russian philosophers into the overall movement of history. It was exhilarating and it was also well made. Yet at the climax of the second play the audience was jarred out of involvement. After Alexander Herzen's son Kolya was killed in a shipping accident at the age of five, Stoppard had given his father a speech in which he argued there was no need to mourn or be upset. We do not ask of a lily that it be built to last. If the child's life had indeed been brief, it was nevertheless no less perfect. 'The death of a child', Herzen is made to say, 'has no more meaning than the death of armies, of nations. Was the child happy while he lived? That is a proper question, the only question.'

Stoppard is a humane and decent writer, so it would be fair to say that I came out of the production seething at his callousness. Why should he want to disfigure his work by building towards such a brutal sentiment? How could a child's life be compared with that of a flower? Really, this was taking the religious view of things too far. Even a priest mourns. However, when talking a few days later to a member of the production team, I was gently put right. The words were not Stoppard's. They were

Herzen's. The dramatist had felt compelled to include them, against many objections, because he had wanted to give full rein to the character's unpredictability. It was a question not just of integrity but of artistic completeness. Stoppard had been taken aback that his hero, whom he so admired in real life, had been so indifferent to the death of his own son. The author had included Herzen's words because they seemed to him so surprising. But nowhere in the coverage of *The Coast of Utopia* did anyone try to belittle it by labelling it as a verbatim play.

You may say that I had committed nothing more than the vulgar crime of ascribing to an author the opinions of one of his or her characters. What a crass mistake for a fellow playwright to have made! But you may also observe that the inconsistent detail, the confounding, non-fitting fact is often the giveaway mark of material drawn from life, rather than the imagination. Herzen's attitude to mortality had struck us all so hard precisely because it seemed so contradictory in such a sensitive man.

In James Marsh's documentary *Man on Wire*, Philippe Petit celebrates his achievement of spending forty-five minutes crossing a steel cable suspended 1,350 feet above Manhattan between the twin towers of the World Trade Center in 1974 by coming down and sleeping with an unknown admirer whom he happens to meet in the street. By doing so, he destroys his long-term relationship with the partner who has helped him plan his feat in the first place. Our response is to exclaim, 'Oh my God, this must be true. It must be true because it's so unlikely.' Or maybe we use that other comforting phrase, so hated by all writers of fiction: 'Nobody could make this up.' Asked for his reasons for making the trip, Petit replied, 'When

I see three oranges, I juggle. When I see two towers, I walk.'
But significantly he omitted to add, 'And when I come down
from two towers, I make love to the first woman I see.'

'Is this true?' 'Is this a true story?' is now the question you
hear asked most frequently in cinemas. Before a film a big card
appears: 'This is based on a true story.' By its very blankness,
the card screams authority. But all too often it also pleads
immunity. It functions as a kind of prophylactic, a way of
protecting the subsequent proceedings from undue criticism.
By declaring in advance that something is true, the film-makers
seek to absolve themselves from the highest demands of art.
The implication is that if it's true, it must be interesting. And if
it's ill-articulated, well then, so is life. The updated CV piously
tacked on at the end of the film – telling us that the tousled
hero is today running a brothel in downtown São Paolo, or
that the lovable heroine overcame her crack habit to open a
small bakery in Montecito, only later to fall victim to dengue
fever, contracted with her new lover in equatorial Africa – is
also intended to ward off our more spontaneous reactions to
the film itself. It aims to douse the flame of any artistic dislike
we may have felt.

However, this flaunting of a project's origins as proof of
its worthiness seems to be more and more prevalent. Whose
heart does not sink at the prospect of yet another series of
half-worked television biopics – not really documentaries,
not really drama – which seek to hitch a ratings ride on our
foreknowledge of, say, Eric Morecambe or Tony Hancock?
Who does not feel compassion for an actor who has responded
to the challenge of portraying Maria Callas by getting down

every one of her physical characteristics except, of course, the ability to sing demanding operatic arias better than anyone else in the world? John Maynard Keynes may have insisted that during a recession it was beneficial to set citizens to work on backbreaking, meaningless labour. They should dig holes in the road and fill them in again. But even Keynes would stop short of asking an Equity member who was not born with Kenneth Williams's rare gifts to make a drama about Kenneth Williams.

Only one time in a hundred does a fictional biography like *Temple Grandin*, HBO's recent account of an autistic teenager whose heightened feeling for cattle led her to design and build humane slaughterhouses all over America, not seem merely a prisoner of its own forewritten narrative. All discerning cinemagoers relish anything from Gus Van Sant, but who can put their hand on their heart and say that his fictionalised film *Milk* has anything like the resonance of Rob Epstein's documentary *The Times of Harvey Milk*, by which it is presumably inspired? Who, indeed, would go to a novelist for the most vivid and comprehensive picture of North America in the last half-century? Who would not go first to Joan Didion's essays?

'You cannot improve on the facts,' said Hilary Mantel, in a ringing defence of accuracy in historical fiction. But Mantel was most certainly not arguing that it was enough to offer only the facts. Nor is it a guarantee of importance in art that the art directs itself to an important subject. I referred at the start to Kenneth Tynan. Every Sunday, like so many other students in the 1960s, I fell out of bed and read him. But his biggest misstep came in the week when he reviewed Peter Watkins's film *The War Game*. Because it speculated on the effects of a nuclear attack on a typical English city, 'it might', said Tynan, 'be the most important film ever made . . . *The War Game* stirred me at a level deeper than panic or grief . . . We are told that works of art cannot change the course of history . . . I believe this one might.' In the context of its screening, Tynan said, it was impossible to take seriously the other films released that week. An Italian director had come up with 'an ecstasy of chic self-indulgence, a gigantic parcel which conceals beneath its gaudy wrapping, a fragment of old rope'. How could anyone bother with 'an immensely pretty film of monumental triviality' when it was placed beside a harrowing vision like *The War Game*?

Now admittedly, *Juliet of the Spirits* is not *La Dolce Vita*. But nor is it nothing. It is a film to which you may return many times for pleasure and instruction. And yet, oddly, in their characteristic mix of autobiography, of fiction and of fantasy, Fellini's films raise the very same question I want to ask tonight. How can there be a wrong way to make good art? And, indeed, what point does criticism serve when it asserts only 'This is not the sort of thing of which I approve'? When a tortured critic like James Wood twists himself into a pretzel struggling to explain exactly why the particular novel he has under review is the wrong kind of good novel, he sounds like nothing so much as a Railtrack official railing against the wrong kind of snow. All the rules dictate that, in *8½*, Fellini ought not to be able to construct a counter-intuitive masterpiece out of his own pampered indecisiveness. But he does.

All over the world serious work is being made in all sorts of unauthorised ways. Opinion, meanwhile, is tying its shoelaces and not noticing. In the face of the evidence, it is still held as an article of faith by high-minded observers that it takes time for artists to absorb events. Any response that appears too quickly must, it is claimed, be journalism, not art. The fact that Wilfred Owen wrote the greatest poems of the First World War in the heat of battle does not shake the prejudice. If the high-minded had their way, Owen would have waited to lend the events more distance. He would, mind you, have been killed in the meanwhile, and his poems would never have got written, but at least Owen would have died with the consolation of knowing that he did at least plan to compose on a critically approved timescale. Addressing a similar conviction – that films about the occupation of Iraq and the war in Afghanistan are bound to be flawed because they lack perspective – the critic David Denby asks this excellent question: 'Box-office wisdom holds that it is too early to make movies about this conflict; but how can it ever be too early to make a good film?'

It is this question of prematurity – 'Hold on, I'm not ready for this' – which bedevils the reception of any work on a contemporary subject. It is very hard in these circumstances to ensure that the question the work provokes is neither 'How soon has it been made?' nor even 'What has it been made from?' but the far more lasting question: 'How deep does it go?' I said earlier that the example for my recent plays had come from Balzac – 'What was it like living under New Labour? How did Tony Blair seem when he went to war?' But I need to make clear that I therefore regard *The Permanent Way*, *Stuff Happens*, *Murder in Samarkand*, *Gethsemane* and *The Power of Yes* as something entirely different from journalism, although they are often mistaken for it.

Journalism is reductive. This is not always the fault of journalists. It is in the nature of the job. At its best and worst, journalism aims to distil. It aims to master, even to subjugate, a particular topic. In this ambition, as every cursory reader of British newspapers will know, the journalist will always run the risk of tipping over into contempt. As soon as something can be summarised it can also be dispatched. Anyone who has ever attended morning conference at a national newspaper will know the form: everyone taking part in the human comedy is a fool. What was once the humorous stance of *Private Eye* has become the humourless stance of the entire press. All politicians are corrupt, all manual workers are idle, all social workers are incompetent, all immigrants are scroungers. The gap between what people are and what they are treated as in journalism has never been wider. Only the very best journalists know how to suggest that a person, theory or event is not just what the journalist believes it to be. It is also itself. Holding that balance between your account and a proper respect for the truth of what something or somebody is outside your account involves a level of self-awareness hard to achieve in 600 words.

In the West a journalistic culture which takes in both the internet and television has become both tiring and ubiquitous. It has also led to a curious deformation in society. As citizens, we consider our family, our friends and, most of all, our children as likeable and virtuous. But we are encouraged to consider everyone we don't know – and most especially those we know only through newspapers or holding any kind of public position – as ridiculous or vicious. To this tendency, this desire to bundle people and thereby to dismiss them, art and death are the most powerful known antidotes.

Art reminds us that things are never quite as simple as they seem. Nor are people. Journalism is life with the mystery taken out. Art is life with the mystery restored. Put people on the stage, in all their humanity, propel them into a course of events and, in even the most savage satire or preposterous farce, characters may acquire a sympathy, a scale, a helplessness, all of which draw forth feelings eerily reminiscent of those elicited by people you actually know.

Meanwhile to the objection that plays and novels about contemporary events are too hastily conceived to be profound is added the confident counter-objection that such works are unlikely to endure. William Shakespeare's plays may be crammed with incomprehensible Elizabethan references and jokes which amuse nobody, and these have hardly damaged his continuing popularity. But the example of literature's highest achiever does little to blunt the popularity of this line of attack. How on earth, it is asked, can either foreign cultures or generations unborn ever be interested in such local doings? On this question, I can only say I am willing to take my chances. Like most writers, I have at best a sceptical attitude to posterity. But wherever playwrights gather, you will find them telling stories of plays, performed in far-off places and years after their premieres, which have acquired what seems like an accidental shimmer.

Of a recent revival of *Stuff Happens* in Canada – six years, remember, after the National Theatre first conceived a then topical account of the lead-up to the Iraq war – the director wrote me a letter: 'I find the play infinitely sadder than a few years ago . . . I think there is something potent about these people now officially out of office and firmly set in their historical place. At the same time, the references to both Afghanistan and Iraq are, this time, eliciting vocal responses from the audiences that I don't recall having happened in my previous production.' In response to such a letter, any playwright will argue two things. First, no proper play is ever just 'about' the events it describes. The whole intention of a play in describing one thing is to evoke another. Although *Stuff Happens* was said to be ripped from the headlines, those who worked on its first production always rested their hopes on its allegorical resonance, its feeling for other processes and for other wars which would take it way beyond the particular path to Iraq. Bush and Blair, after all, are not the only two warmongers in history. But, secondly, in celebrating this play's bewildering success in Toronto six years on, the director was, in fact, celebrating the special nature of theatre itself.

In Stalinist Russia, the most powerful protest you could make was to stage *Hamlet*.

As early as 2006 Sarah Palin stood as the independent candidate for the governorship of Alaska. Andrew Halcro was first to observe of Sarah Palin that she had what any politician would kill for: 'And that is the ability to make substance irrelevant.' Theatre has the very opposite ability. It finds substance out, and weighs it with devastating accuracy. But when deeply felt, theatre also has, like the music of Delius and Elgar, the potential to inflame the imagination of others.

When *The Power of Yes* opened last October in Angus Jackson's production, it laid out the progress of the current banking crisis.

It was inevitable that the immediate response be journalistic. It either was or wasn't accurate. Its diagnosis was or wasn't correct. The play suggested that bankers have come to constitute the most powerful trade union in the world, dedicated to their own interests, and indifferent to yours or mine. This proposition was received either with outrage or delight. The play further argued that bankers have the upper hand over anyone elected to power, firstly because complicated financial practices are beyond the understanding of most democratic politicians, but secondly because bankers have refined all their various blackmail notes into one single threat, recently left like a bomb in a litter bin: 'If you don't rig the market in our favour, we will drag you down with us.' The legitimacy of such intellectual terrorism was also hotly debated – on both sides.

Thus far, the issues raised by *The Power of Yes* might well have been batted back and forth on a lively edition of *Newsnight*. Because the play portrayed real people, and used their actual dialogue, so the dish arrived ready spiced for journalistic carving. But then, interestingly, a second wave of reaction followed, which addressed not so much the play's ideas as its techniques for deploying those ideas. Many things were expected of a play about high finance, but it was not foreseen that it should resemble Michael Bennett's production of *A Chorus Line*. Friends reported that they found the sight of twenty suited bankers lining up across the proscenium arch curiously moving. From then on, nothing was as they'd anticipated, least of all their own responses.

Many spectators noticed that this was an unusual example of a verbatim play which did not seem set on righting a wrong.

It did not demand the reform of the banking system, nor even, indeed, offer a rallying point for the anger against it. Verbatim theatre was, they thought, a known genre, often a touch hectoring and solemn, at its worst even self-righteous and overly dependent on direct address. On this occasion a resolute attempt was being made to jazz it, to take it places it had never been. A few smart people were clever enough to guess that the inspiration had indeed come from Glenn Gould's radio programmes, which he made over a ten-year period from 1967 onwards. In what became known as the *Solitude Trilogy*, Gould recorded the impressions of Northern Canadians, many of them living lives of extreme isolation, and then sent their voices spinning like music, weaving them, fugue-like, into something the pianist called tapestry.

The most interesting reaction of all came from a painter friend, who had seen as much as he'd listened. In particular, he had enjoyed how much the look of the play resembled an installation by Bill Viola. Short, he said, of dropping a violent cascade of water onto the actors' heads, it was Bill Viola. A stage language of light, form and colour had been created by the ravishing projections of Jon Driscoll, the daring of the set designer Bob Crowley and by the restless fluency of the lighting designer Paule Constable. How strange, said my painter friend, that an ostensibly prosaic, ostensibly factual play should unleash some of the purest visual poetry he had ever seen in a theatre.

It is safe to say that I was more flattered by this response than I would have been forty years previously. When I set out in the theatre, I was part of a fringe movement which often sought to crash the problem of aesthetics by doing plays as badly as possible. Or at least as crudely as possible. If you made no attempt to do things overly well, people would not be distracted from what you were saying. In those days, there were Brownie points only for subject matter. But as the years went by, it became clear to me that I had not understood aesthetics at all. Aesthetics were not principally about good and bad. They were not your enemy. They were your opportunity. Style was the means by which you could suggest that what you were writing about was something more than what you appeared to be writing about. Without style there was no suggestiveness, and with no suggestiveness, no metaphor. The processes of art could begin nowhere else.

'Are you the notorious composer Arnold Schoenberg?' someone once asked of Arnold Schoenberg. His reply has gone down in history. 'Yes. Somebody had to be.' In the last few years, I admit I have felt a mild degree of fellow feeling. 'Are you the person who makes plays out of what's going on in the papers?' is never a question asked in a friendly manner. Nor is the answer much liked. 'Yes. Somebody has to.'

'How on earth do I review that?' said the theatre critic of one prominent national daily, crying out to a colleague as he left the first night of *The Power of Yes*. It is as if the doors of our theatre, of their own volition, blow shut all the time, and the task is always to prise them back open. Plenty of people get their poetry from science, from the physical universe, from the contemplation of mathematics, or of animals, or of solitude or of the stars. An audience arrives fearing the theatre to be one more medium like any other. If the subject of the play comes from political life, they anticipate a form of animated journalism, journalism on legs, the usual mud soup of opinion and sociology. But, in fact, the performing arts can deliver high-flying bankers who are at once contemptible and sympathetic.

The motive behind this lecture is to point out that the word 'factual' is not synonymous with the word 'prosaic'. If we accept the simple distinction that factual work asks questions for us, whereas fictional work is more likely to ask questions of us, there is no reason why some work may not do both. What matters to any artist is not where you find your materials, but where you go with them. Writing about public events may well involve an act of imagination just as profound, just as transformative as for any other kind of art. And the results will be as emotionally involving. The highfalutin prejudice against any such category is misconceived. But it is only the flip-side of an opposite assumption, which is equally damaging. Having recently presented to a television company a film in which at least two of the three principal characters were alcoholic, I was asked the following questions.

Q: What is this based on?
A: Nothing.
Q: Who are these people meant to be?
A: Nobody.
Q: Who are they then?
A: They're fictional.
Q: Are you alcoholic yourself?
A: No.

Q: Then why did you write it?

A: Because the philosophical implications of addiction are fascinating to me.

Q: Do you think we should have a helpline number at the end for anyone who watches this film and is disturbed by it?

A: No.

The single fictional film has become such an endangered species on television that the automatic assumption is that it can only be a posh version of current affairs and nothing else. Nothing confuses a BBC executive more than the words 'I made it up'.

Anyone contemplating the best cinema of the twenty-first century is going to notice an extraordinary resurgence in social realism, whether in Cristian Mungiu's *4 Months, 3 Weeks and 2 Days*, in the Dardenne brothers' *L'Enfant* or in *Un Prophète* by Jacques Audiard. But although these three outstanding films, one from Romania, one from Belgium, the last from France, all deceive the audience into thinking they are watching something lifelike, underneath they are as deeply worked, as thoroughly imagined and as wholly invented as anything by Poussin or Henry James. All three boast classical plots disguised under everyday surfaces. The need for an illegal abortion, the sale of a newborn baby by his indigent father, and the rise of a young Arab criminal taking power from a Corsican gang in a French prison all provide mainsprings for stories of impoverishment in which willpower battles against fate as inexorably as in any courtly tragedy.

Gillo Pontecorvo's film *The Battle of Algiers* was made in 1966, but it was projected in The Pentagon in 2003 for the benefit of officers and strategic experts planning the occupation of Iraq. Intended to describe one situation, it illuminated another. Its portrayal of guerrilla war in Algeria in the 1950s proved relevant to another attritional fight in the following century. Flyers inviting military experts to the screening were headlined 'How to win a battle against terrorism and lose the war of ideas'. But, again, Pontecorvo had disguised his strategies as documentary.

Even that most conservative of cultural critics, T. S. Eliot, confessed that you cannot contribute to a tradition unless you are determined to extend it. 'What happens when a new work of art is created is something that happens simultaneously to all the works of art that preceded it.' At the moment, a handful of us are attracted to mixing fiction and reality in unfamiliar ways. *Stuff Happens* is referred to as a documentary play, but two-thirds of it is made up. George W. Bush and Tony Blair did not invite me to carry a tape recorder with them into the woods at Crawford, Texas, in April 2002, when they first conceived the momentous plan to occupy Iraq. Indeed, they did not invite anyone. There were no witnesses. To this day, nobody knows for sure what happened. I had to invent their encounter from my imagination, pretty much as Schiller invented Mary Stuart's encounter with Elizabeth I – with the sole proviso that some version of the Blair–Bush meeting did actually occur.

'Aren't you telling us what we already know?' is the last question, always aimed between my eyes, potentially lethal in the questioner's view, but not even causing a skin wound when fired. 'No, I am not. You may think you know about something. But it's one thing to know, and another to experience.' The paradox of great factual work is that it restores wonder. Thinly imagined work takes it away.

'I never knew that, I never realised that, I never felt that' is what you hear from the departing audience when their evening has been well spent. Because we think we know, but we don't.

(2010)

POEMS

WE TRAVELLED

We travelled
We travelled for this, taking it with us
In the back of the van
And believing, however far we had to go
That we were taking something good
Something worthwhile
Early in the travels, in the late nineteen sixties,
I started sketching a map in my diary of motorway cafés
We ate salmon-pink sausages and fat dead slabs
Of pig between springy slices of bread
Every day, every night, late at night
Because we had something good
Something worthwhile
We threw a cat's cradle across the UK
We left towns, all of us hooting with laughter
At the upset we had caused
And, as we believed, the truths we had told
And so passed the next fifty years
Minus so much travel
But including the good

*

The night I saw Michael Bennett's production
Of *Dreamgirls* in a theatre in New York
I remember thinking
No art form comes near

Because at its best it's dizzying
On evenings like that, unspoken ideas melted
Into emotions
You couldn't tell them apart
People afterwards didn't even know how to talk
Because of the breathlessness you feel
When you take your heart for a walk
I believed in it

Of all my battlegrounds I liked the Olivier best
Because it was the most martial
Allowing for nothing but war and story
It made no concessions to mood
No mood possible except the mood
Of things happening

'Theatre's just tat,' said Howard
Very early on, one day in the van,
'How can you say you love theatre? What do you love?
Chipboard, spackle and nails? Because that's all it is.'

*

The performance culture I entered was
Elaborate, defined.
It was sharply tiered,
Like mille-feuille.
It was structured, refined.
At the top, the famous actors and dramatists
Who dazzled the audiences with the skills
Which they had inherited

From actors and dramatists before them
Patiently, they worked their way up
Today the hierarchy is gone
The skills are gone
Everything's about everything
We all agree
And nothing's about anything

'Speak up, please, I can't hear you
Speak up!
Please!'

*

Why did I imagine
A life spent making things up
Would help anyone
When it turned out that my country
Was set like a plough, only a few
Degrees wrong after the war
But by the time it had crossed the field
After seventy years
Half a mile askew
At entirely the wrong point
Diagonally
Where nobody had once
Set out to be
'How did we get here?
What the hell are we doing here?'

*

At the beginning
We travelled so many miles
In the dark
Careering home
Too poor to stay in hotels
Too cheap to eat in restaurants
Too happy to care

One early morning
Heading back towards London
The van turned over
One and a half times
Like a tumble dryer
And the actors
Were odd socks inside
Afterwards, waiting for rescue,
They sat on the verge
Both shocked and not shocked
Because they were thinking
'That was bound to happen
That was always going to happen'

*

When the Romans built a theatre
They had to decide on its size
They counted the population
Of the town
Then divided by ten
That's how many people

They expected each night
One-tenth of the town
OK, we expected no one
And were grateful for anyone
And if no one came
We went to the pub instead
Unconcerned
Not even thinking
'Is this the right choice?
Is this the best life to live?'

*

It's harder now
Because the democracy of voices
Prefers that nothing be too
Outstandingly good
The playwrights of my youth
Were usually drunks
Vicious ornery unkind
Ready to pick a fight
Ready to take offence
At an imagined slight
Determined to insist
That the only value was 'I myself'
'I alone'
In the face of the ubiquity of commerce
Which was, they claimed,
Trying to make everyone the same
They despised money, career, fame

Seeing the future laid out before them
The drunken dramatists screamed
As if trapped behind glass
They were not easy people to be with
Storming out of rooms
Denouncing colleagues
Jumping to their feet
At misheard insults
In love with
The too-easy pleasure of
Losing control
But let's remember
At some personal cost
They defied the crowd
Now writers are expected
To express the crowd
Not to defy it

*

Somewhere in the distance
A lift is falling
Falling ever faster to the ground
And inside it, the work of a generation

*

I'm lying on a lawn in Florence
Admiring the Tuscan hills
Looking down to the Ponte Vecchio
With Howard again
And a friend from the fringe

The whole world before us
It's 1975
And we're discussing happily
Where to have lunch
Later the international conference report
Will say, 'The English delegation
Seemed happier sunning themselves
Drinking Chianti
And eating pasta
Than discussing The Future of the Theatre'

How few people understand
Life isn't what you intend
It's what you do

*

At its worst
Theatre isn't challenge
It's piety
It's church
Everyone joining together
To be confirmed
In what we already believe
How often I've wanted to shout
From the stalls
'Yes I know this
I know this
It's what's currently believed.'
As much at my own work, mind you,
As at anyone else's

*

And yet theatre kept pulling me back
I can't say why
As I changed partners
Changed marriages
Changed countries
Changed lives
There it was
Always
The nearest thing to a root
A base
From which I set out
And to which I returned
Reality firmly fixed in unreality
Ready and waiting for me
At least until now
Something's changed
Probably it isn't the theatre
Probably it's me

*

I'm dispatching an idea into the auditorium
It can't be seen, it can't be said
It's not in the words
And it's not in the action either
If you were asked how it happened
You couldn't necessarily say
And yet there it is

*

I don't feel any sadness
About misplacing my love for it
It's something that's slipped past
Without my noticing
One day walking towards the playhouse
With excitement
The next day not
Feeling restless
Like a tennis player
Who's tried every shot
I'm not disillusioned
Because I was never illusioned
I was simply blithe
With the glamour
Of changing people's
Angle of view
Alongside discovering
My own too

I look on with envy
With pleasure
To this day
I look with delight
Of course I do
What joy!
The young are setting off
In vans
To cover the country
They're travelling

DECEMBER 1991

She drove me to Trouville in her black Volkswagen drop-top
Leaving Paris early by the Périphérique and getting there
    by noon
There was frost even on the inside of the slanted back window
And the laughable so-called heater pretty soon

Gave out. The tyres rocked on the brittle brown concrete.
The car shook. The frozen air thickened like a knife,
Pellucid, and we left a trail of hot breath through Northern
    France.
As we travelled I thought 'New life.'

New life. Deauville went by, with its curious timbered
    medieval
Travesty of a hotel. Thank God we're not lunching there.
We prefer to head for white-tiled, cheap and cheerful,
A neon-lit, salty lunch at Les Vapeurs where

Our idea of what is good, pithy little peppered shrimp
    and oysters,
Dredged from the bed, sole, chips, beer, coincided. 'Oh this
    is what she likes.'
The mud-brown beach stretching away beyond
And the silver sea motionless, trapped, unchanging, painted;
    estuaries, dykes

Small boats, dredgers abandoned, the weather
Too raw for anyone, however calloused by experience,
   to pass red hands over rope.
This is the place, bracing then, where I find what it turns out
   I've been looking for,
By the sand, by the water, the what-you-don't-even-know-
   you're-missing: hope.

OCTOBER NIGHTS

As it happened, I'd been for a parents' evening
    at Lewis's school near St Paul's
His teachers as usual were all giving him a brilliant report
I was going from one to another at small tables, each
    outdoing the last in their praises
Hell! How could I possibly have a son who's so popular,
    I thought

As I walked away, down past the old Mermaid Theatre, as was,
When I myself had made such a thoroughgoing mess
    of so much:
Wrecked marriage, countless unequal relationships, beds left
    at dawn. Power distributed
Badly, messily. Too much 'Who wants what?' and 'I've had
    enough.' Call it a faultless touch

For giving and taking offence. My father dead. Passing up
    to Ludgate Circus and on to Fleet Street
The Strand. Gathering pace. Am I late? Overwhelmed with
    feelings of failure and shame
That awful film, the play that didn't work, the day I lost my
    temper at nothing.
No escape. You are who you are. Or so it seems. Is everyone
    the same?

Across Trafalgar Square and from the pubs and bars,
    laughter so loud I was thinking:
Can anything really be that funny or are they pretending?
Still I've got a date with a fashion designer waiting
    in a restaurant and that's not something
Many people can say. Some compensation with luck
    for the unending

Self-questioning of a personality I've never quite been able
    to trust.
Up St James's, past the gentlemen's clubs full of armchairs,
    and the sumptuous October night
Fills me with excitement. The plate-glass window. The blinds.
    The table in the corner. She's there.
Mr Do Everything Wrong is about to become Mr Do
    Something Right

COUP DE FOUDRE

If there were any way of expressing what I felt when I first saw
    Nicole Farhi, then I would have found it by now
I remember the instant of looking between us because she was
    laughing like a *ragazza* at the other side of the room
Not for a moment did it seem likely that a bronzed
    mop-haired Italian could be interested in someone
    like me but I thought I'd go and ask anyway

She says my questions were amazingly direct and impertinent
    – 'Where do you live? Do you live alone?' – but it seems
    unusual for me to have been so straight-to-the-point
I often place her in the room geographically at a different
    angle from the spot where she believes herself to have been
And in the remembering the person beside her has changed
    many times, sometimes her friend Maite, sometimes Sarah
    Hodsoll, and at times even someone else entirely

There isn't going to be another night like this and
    the restaurant has since changed its decor probably
    hoping that the customers will forget its gruelling cuisine
It's as if someone has come along and deliberately wiped
    the blackboard to remove all trace of the place
But there it is in my mind, still dark, still strangely carpeted,
    with a woman I've never seen before looking as though she
    already knows me, or if she doesn't, would like to

You don't get these very often, do you? these moments
     on which your life hinges and which you recognise
     obscurely as they happen
Next day after fifteen minutes' conversation I wrote
     in my diary 'I have met a woman and I have the
     ridiculous feeling my future happiness depends on her'
Generally, I am academically clever and emotionally
     quite stupid but on this occasion I can boast a modest
     degree of prescience, and that's understating it

The mistake is to think that days go by sequentially,
     and because there's such a thing as a calendar so there
     must be an obvious progress, 'This happens one day,
     then this the next'
But what about those events which take place outside time,
     which fly above it, and in whose perspective all else is seen,
     as if sequence itself were unimportant
It was like being lifted up and offered an aerial view: I met
     Nicole Farhi and everything changed

TWO PEOPLE PASS IN THE STREET

Two people pass in the street who years ago used to make love
Now they look away
She has a particular way, knowing he's seen her, knowing
    she's been seen –
A particular way of becoming invisible

Also – years ago, talking to the famous director
Who was no longer friends with the older playwright
'You're too young. I can't explain.
All I can tell you: it becomes impossible.'

'Impossible'? Isn't 'impossible' putting it high?

It's comfortable, isn't it, to live on a grid of memory
Walking the city streets
'This is where I met her
  – Look, that café where we said goodbye'
Oh, they're markers, aren't they, buoys,
The yellow kind, with flags on them,
The cheap plastic flags round which you navigate, or else
    you're disqualified
Life's a regatta, all right, or the thought of it is, at least
Half a mile out to sea
Sailing by

'Am I too quick?' 'Do you like this?' 'Shall I do it again?'
What's going on in the bed twenty years earlier?
What are the chances of knowing when neither knew
    at the time?
'I'm sorry.'
'I didn't mean that.'
'I'm sorry.'
'If you don't mind, I'm getting up early in the morning.'

Downstairs in the basement I remember the cancer
    nurse coming
The sound of her climax, extravagant, like opera,
    from the flat below
And the pigeons ascending, beating their wings
    at the sound of her
Thrilling to her
The palliative day, the long pastoral day put behind her –
Release at last!
Out into the air. Like song. My God, the sound of her!

'The past doesn't exist,' says Wally.
'It certainly isn't here, and it isn't anywhere else, as far as
    I can see.'

Beat the drum of action easy
Stay the heart and its advance
Take the measure of the music
Stop before you join the dance

Hold on till the last cadenza
Hold on till the last embrace
Full of fear, confusion, mystery
Cross the road, avoid the place

A WEEKEND IN ST PETERSBURG

Looking at what happened to Akhmatova
There isn't any way, is there, any of us could add anything?
Visit her domestic museum in St Petersburg
And you will find the record of a life lived in an enfilade
    of small rooms –
Unfortunate to fall in love with a man
With a wife already
But what followed was rather more than unfortunate

The Fountain Palace is now opposite a parade of shops
Shops, as you understand, being the mark of freedom
We press our noses to the window
We like the idea of looking in on Akhmatova's suffering
Because she was beautiful, romantic and survived

Better to be a tourist in her life than to live it
Her experience is now at a suitable distance

Later, at dinner, Shostakovich's son is opposite,
    eating mackerel
Completely uninterested in anyone around him
A distant descendant of Tchaikovsky is making a speech
Nearby, the famous conductor Gergiev has two mobiles
One for each ear
While managing some lamb chops at the same time

So much that is terrible has passed through this city
Blown through this city
Like a dust of unbeing
And here the relics remain talking only to each other

IMPERFECT VILLANELLE

I can see too clearly I'm getting to the close
The sun at the window has lost its heat
You may not speak of it but everyone knows

It happens much faster than we might suppose
Our idea of the future is in sure retreat
I can see too clearly I'm getting to the close

Temperaments formed as our fortunes rose
May prove unsuited to imminent defeat
You may not speak of it but everyone knows

The careless control we could once impose
Now reads more nearly as pure conceit
I can see too clearly I'm getting to the close

With the passage of time foreboding grows
We give one performance and no repeat
You may not speak of it but everyone knows

This is the feeling when idealism goes
Set down my dreams at my enemy's feet
I can see too clearly I'm getting to the close
You may not speak of it but everyone knows

FOR REG

In Memory of Reg Gadney 1941–2018

Who can see the pattern?
Not him
He's remarkably cheerful
I leave him in good spirits

This is not going to end well

What did he find down there?
Under the knife
Something he feared
Worse than anything he'd seen
And yet he came back up
Chewing toffees he'd bought
On the internet
A particular toffee that pleased him
It was enough to please him

This is not going to end well

He loved telling stories
But never told them the same way twice
Because he never remembered them
The same way twice

Everything in Reg was flux
Everything was change

We walked together forty years ago
In a field in Cambridgeshire
Laughing together about
The shaming levels of self-deception
Necessary to living
We walked in the corn, roaring with laughter
Our lives in a house way to the west
And not yet seeing
That these levels lower
Towards the end

Much more known, nothing forgotten

Everything that ever happened
At last in a single bed
Unavailable to be changed

At the last we're fixed

I'm losing you Reg
You're becoming definitive

This has not ended well

XX – NICOLE

She has bread and olives for breakfast
That's if there are no fish-eggs or herrings left in the fridge
If there's a documentary on television about animals
Then she will watch it
And a calm will come upon her
As if she lived among animals and was happy among them
If she sees a sleeve on an old coat, then she's one of only
    six people in the world who know how to put it on
    a different coat
And make of the sleeve, and of the coat, something new
She transforms them
A French-Turkish alchemist with a savoury tooth

When she argues with her mother, then both of them know
    they are right
And they use argument not to argue but to reinforce their
    original positions
This comes from confidence

'Don't interrupt,' she'll say, 'I'm getting to the end of my book
I want to know how the story ends'
She's never sure at the beginning
'I'm not sure I like it'
But later, when she's deeper in, she goes as deep as you can go
The same calm
She gives in to a good pair of hands

She gives in and is fulfilled
'What a great story! That was a good book!'

Nobody quite understands where her sureness comes from
She says her parents but she's guessing

She is without any practical sense of direction
Because she so clearly believes she doesn't need one
She will find what she wants, when she wants it
So it never occurs to her to look in advance

A stranger to machines and instructions, she proceeds
    by intuition
Where the rest of us use maps

When the car runs out of petrol, she prefers to say it has
    'broken down'

I still wear the coat she gave me in the week we met
    twenty years ago
And I'll always wear it
Because I remember walking round London as if
    I were wearing her

FOREIGN TRAVEL

I love how she falls asleep when she gets on the plane
She sits in her seat and at once
She closes her eyes and she's happy. She's at peace
So often she's been beside me in the last twenty-five years
As the jets took hold and the ground was left behind

We were always going somewhere

When we got to the destination she was often disappointed
It wasn't exactly what she had in mind
As though the job of reality were to conform
    to her imagination
Rather than, as most of us expect, vice versa

Then she starts to merge into her surroundings

I've never been anywhere where she didn't belong
She looked dead right up Machu Picchu
And in Shanghai, eating dumplings, she didn't look foreign
    at all
Admittedly she vomited on top of the volcano
In the Atacama Desert
But she still managed to look chic on the way up
On the New York subway she's one more passenger
And the sheer rock face of Mount Cook

Seems to have been designed to show her to best advantage
Look at her heel at a natural angle dug into the snow

All her life she's popped up everywhere

I took her walking in Patagonia and on a thin ridge,
    quite high,
Between two green hilltops
The wind tried to blow her off and failed
I wouldn't have feared for her because she would have
    floated down, serene

Everything seems so close from this perspective

THOMAS GAINSBOROUGH

The Gainsborough Museum in Sudbury
Needs a portrait of Thomas Gainsborough
Because they don't have one
So cleverly they ask my wife
Who comes up with one in a matter of days

When she hands it over, at once they ask her for ten

How does she do it?
I'd say it's nothing to do with likeness
More to do with the aura
Because if you look at Gainsborough's features
As they really were
They weren't very interesting

He becomes interesting in my wife's portrait

What is this gift she has?
Did she see something in his face which I didn't see?
Or did she put it there?
More likely after a sleep of just two hundred and fifty years
Poor Thomas Gainsborough stirred himself, swelled slightly
Pulled himself together, did the very best he could
For the occasion, thinking:
'I'd better make an effort for Nicole

Because if I show my best side
It'll be worth it, I'll be rewarded'

That's the effect she has

It isn't just the dead who try harder when she's around
I do too

CLAY

Your thumbs make faces, your fingers eyes
Behind the skin, the person lies
Latent. The lumpy mould of clay relies

On you. The shape is there,
Sturdy. Your thumbs make chins, your fingers hair
In threads. The basic attitude is fair,
The crack right through the skull, despair.

My sculptress wife steps back, surveys
She passes long, transforming days
At last the material yields, obeys,

Submits. Stop work! Leave it! Leave it now!
It's done. Risk more work, it's gone.
Your thumbs make fingers, your fingers ears
The soul emerges, hovers, disappears

PARTY GIVING

I've always been frightened of giving a party
Because I've always been certain no one will come
As I look round the room, I'm solely aware
Not of who's present but of who's not there

I'm not liked. So why should anyone bother?
On my fortieth birthday my girlfriend forgot to attend
Or was it deliberate? I've had time to reflect
Was she intending to hurt, or was it far more likely neglect?

Carpet stains, Twiglets, warm wine left over for months
Raised voices, abandon, music, hysteria, waste
I'm left with a suspicion I can't control
It's not a celebration, it's an opinion poll

SAY WHAT YOU LIKE

Say what you like about the playwright
But at least he had the good sense
To be born after World War Two
And to leave before World War Three got under way

Say what you like about the playwright
But he never belonged to any club
He played all the golf he was going to play before he was forty
He never wore blue jeans
He lived in his wife's house
And he kept his cars for as long as they went on working

It wasn't snobbery
Nor was it thinking himself better than anyone else
More the knowledge that he'd lucked into a period in which
    nothing much was going to happen
At least to him

Around him the world was a slum of injustice and inequality
And on this injustice he made not the slightest impression
His plays were performed in countries where citizens were
    regularly arrested
Or disappeared
But the performance of his plays continued in their absence

His plays were 'important' to him

Oh yes, say what you like about the playwright
At six foot one he was able to see to the far side of the room
But when he travelled his ignorance of languages
Left him unable to understand much of what was said to him

Across the carpet of his study the thread was worn where
    his feet paced every day
And he sat at the desk he was given when he first became
    a writer
Occasionally foreign students came to his studio because
    it had once been occupied by a minor painter of the
    London School
Who had wrestled with another painter, who had refused
    to have sex in the bed immediately above where the
    playwright now worked

There was a plaque to that effect

For over forty years he wrote consistently
Without becoming an adjective like Pinter
Nor even a national treasure like Alan Bennett
When the time came round each year for Public Lending
    Right royalties
He usually found not many of his books had been borrowed
    from libraries
He felt that while he was writing at least he was alone
And so he couldn't hurt anyone else

It's murderers who say 'Yes I killed him but think
    how many I spared'

Say what you like about the playwright
But something worked out for him
Because his wife was a good person
And his children grew up to be honest and forthright

Did they feel implicated in his failure? How do I know?

OLD FILMS

All old films are more interesting than
All new
Even Rock Hudson
Unlikely crossing the Alps
In *A Farewell to Arms*
Fascinates
In a way Keira Knightley can't possibly
As Colette

It's not her fault
Nor is it just that Rock Hudson won't be papped tonight
In Soho House necking a Negroni

All old films send a message from the past
About how people thought differently and are now
Impenetrable

We've let go their hand and they're falling

Barbara Stanwyck, Françoise Dorléac, Myrna Loy
Have a thickness to their experience
Which Jack Nicholson doesn't

Is it distance which lends enchantment
Or – what I think – were they more interesting
In the first place?

RUE DES ÉCOLES

My favourite street in Paris is the Rue des Écoles
Because it has so many repertory cinemas
On Thursday we watched Ozu's *Floating Weeds*,
Ava Gardner in *The Killers* and Jean-Louis Trintignant
Acting perfectly in *Violent Summer*
With Eleanora Rossi Drago

I'd never heard of Drago before but
Sensual, the flame of intelligence burning bright
In her
She could well have had
Sophia Loren's career. Just bad luck she didn't

It says on the internet she died in 2007

Don't for a moment imagine it's all senior citizens
    in the Rue des Écoles
It isn't
The audience is interestingly mixed in age
In background and in colour
Because, during the pandemic, cinema has mistakenly
Tried to restart with a bummer called *Tenet*
A template of modern indifference
The film-maker as clumsy as we are
And people of all ages parade the strip between
The Champollion and the Grand Action

Longing for something less pompous
And less full of itself

We're looking for something here, all of us,
Something we've lost
It has nothing to do with nostalgia
Nor with completism
Nor with scholarship
Nor even with mere curiosity

More to do with feeling that Audrey Hepburn
May be more vivid than we are
Certainly in *Love in the Afternoon*, trying to deal with
Gary Cooper's backward stupidity
Hepburn's more full of feeling
Asking more
Needing more

Yes, this is the best street in Paris
Haunted by Naruse and Ida Lupino and Billy Wilder
I feared these films were sailing away
Condemned to be remembered only by people
Who drank Kia-Ora and Bovril and read the *Dandy*

But the continued existence of this
Counter-intuitive promenade in Paris
Cheers me more than the birds at dawn
Or the setting sun

Today it's John Garfield in *He Ran All the Way*
Unable to believe that Shelley Winters
May be in love with him

'Garfield?' 'John Garfield?' Yes, but if you can believe it,
His funeral in Hollywood was the best attended
Since Valentino's
He was due to take the part of Terry Malloy
In *On the Waterfront*
But because he died, aged thirty-nine, Marlon Brando
Took his place and played it instead

Perhaps that's why we give ourselves
So unreservedly
We can see the shape of their lives
But we can't see the shape of our own
Because they have story
Because they have form
We look up to dead actors
From the pit of a Paris street
Livelier exemplars than us

More alive

INFLUENCE

For G.B.

'Who are your influences?' the interviewer asks, as though
There were the foggiest chance that I might know.
I long ago mastered the rudiments of the game
But surely no two players then play the same?

Drop shot, lob, forehand, backhand, second service, smash,
Patrol the baseline, define your territory before you do
    anything rash
The rhythms of control become unconscious after a while
Yes, you can learn technique, but how can anyone teach
    you style?

'Surely you admire someone special?' the interviewer says
But no good player expects to play exactly how Federer plays.
They can't. Of course I like Chekhov, Ibsen, O'Casey,
    O'Neill.
They're great. But, sorry, it's a given, I can't feel how they feel.

Nor would I wish to. I don't work in their slipstream. It's clear
A playwright can't hear dialogue with a borrowed ear
The purpose is not to emulate another woman or man
Why not just write as well as you possibly can?

And only you. That's the point. Why else would I bother
To write my play if I meant its fate to be to echo another?
Feeling desperate, feeling hopeless, I can only repeat
'What are your influences?' 'People, history, the street.'

THE ACTOR

In memory of Philip Seymour Hoffman 1967–2014

The actor who we were told is dead is not dead
He's there at the curtain call
In spite of killing himself only five minutes earlier
We're in the well-known world of 'As if'
Did we really believe he was dead?
Of course not
But the actor had spent a diligent evening working towards
    making us feel what we would feel if he were
He deployed his considerable training and his vast experience
    came into play
He managed by the skilful deployment of silences to let us
    imagine we could see into his mind
A huge number of words were also used to achieve this effect
And some beautiful music, which had originated in
    a different production fifty years ago

Now at the curtain call he must choose between telling us we
    should be grave because he's dead or happy because he's not
For the actor, we can see clearly, it's the trickiest acting
    of the evening

SHAKESPEAREAN WEATHER

When Shakespeare wants to make you sit up he always
    draws attention to the weather
The storm in *Lear* is to say we're powerless
And then in *The Tempest*, he summons up another storm
    and this time the message from the writer is 'I'm off'
'Very like a whale' they say in *Hamlet*
It's as if Shakespeare's always looking upwards
'The rain, it raineth every day'
'So fair and foul a day I have not seen'

I'm only pointing this out, but the poet of the so-called
    human –
What did someone call him? 'The inventor of the human' –
Is always looking just as hard at what's now called
    the environment
But what I'd call what we're born into, our surroundings,
    our element

How changeable he is, our poet
And how changeable the climate
What bad weather he endures
How vulnerable he is and how catastrophic

It matters where you are born, Shakespeare says, it makes
     a difference
And it makes a difference where you are and when
And in what conditions

Praise to the man who attends to the external world
Just a slight change in the air, a drop of pressure, and now
     it's snow

WHY DOES SHE THINK IT'S ME?

Why does she seem to think it's me
The woman on the corner
Who's staring at me as if it were my fault

I really don't think it was me who got her into this mess
Although I can see it may well be my job to get her out of it

I'm in Notting Hill where I do remember
People pop up seeming to reproach me
As if I could help them
So many people thrown to the side of the road
Onto the pavement
What am I meant to do?

In Kurosawa's film *Stray Dog*
A policeman has his gun stolen by a criminal
And from then on the detective always feels
That everyone who's killed with it is his responsibility

It's someone else's finger but it's still his gun

I can't carry the sins of the world and nor can you
I've done far too much wrong far too often
I don't understand the real harm I have done
I can't also take on general blame for the state of the world

Or for the woman on the corner
Whose newspapers rustle as she turns on her cardboard
    mattress
And looks straight at me

CALLING ACROSS THE TUNDRA

Trying to explain the sixties to my children at dinner
Is a bit of a ridiculous undertaking
Because anything I say makes me sound like an idiot
'But did people really believe there was going to be
     a revolution?'
'Was it different in France?'
'Why was it different in France?'
'Did May '68 start in the Renault factory?'
'Where is the Renault factory?'
'Why did de Gaulle go to Colombey-les-Deux-Églises?'
'Where is Colombey-les-Deux-Églises?'

All the time I'm trying to explain exactly how we felt
     and why we felt it
My wife is complaining that the dog is always hungry
This is somehow my fault
I don't give her enough to eat
So while I further explain that we once believed
     in the irrevocable need to tear down the institutions
     of the state because they were rotten
Nicole gives the dog another meal
But out of the corner of my eye, as I talk interminably,
     I notice the dog is begging again
I turn to my wife
'Look you give her a second supper and she's still hungry'

PRAISE

Praise is salt water
My throat is sore
I'm getting thirstier
Hang on. Give me more

Tell me I'm great
I get ten seconds' relief
Give me a bucket to
Hydrate my self-belief

It's not working
I'm panicking now
I thought I'd be better
I'm worse – and how

All right, ignore me
Just go away
Let me self-medicate
Please if I may

Oh, next it's abuse
OK, fine. Abuse I'll own
I should have realised
We stand alone

KAY KENDALL PLAYS THE TRUMPET
UNDERGROUND

'With Christ, which is far better' says the gravestone.
It's a quote, from someone, maybe you know who.
I'll relieve the tension. It's from a letter:
Paul, Philippians, somewhere deep in chapter two.

Not that I had known it. Hampstead graveyard
Is quite a mad melange. It's a human potpourri:
Joan Collins' mum, Hugh Gaitskell, Anton Walbrook
And Our Lady guards the bones of Beerbohm Tree.

The flashest grave of all is for Kay Kendall,
The star's last billing: 'Beloved wife of Rex',
And at once you think of *Genevieve* and trumpets,
Of the fifties, tabletops and sex.

Fact is, there's nothing to be said for dying early
Not even in this green, upmarket lot.
Can't really see the point of dying ever.
To be with Christ far better? I think not.

FINNSKY

For my grandson, Finn

Little Finnsky has his arms wide open wide above his head
    as he sleeps on his back
As though saying welcome to all-comers
During the day he says only 'Look' and 'Wow' not much else
An ever-smiling Finnsky soon enough discovers

His native curiosity, delighted, interpreting.
The world isn't yet ready to show Finnsky everything it's got
But this two-year-old's alert – look at those shining eyes –
Under his perfect halo of golden hair he's not

Ever going to distrust anything that's proposed.
His father was known as being fearless on skis
And from Lewis he's inherited a propensity to take risks
So all I can say to him is 'Please

Learn some fear, Finnsky. Not enough to spoil things but
Enough to stop you doing anything stupidly rash.
After all, Finnsky, you're already out in front because
    of your inborn mix
Of humour, gentleness, consideration, warmth and dash.'

OUR HOUSE IN FRANCE

Our house in France is like life
Impossible to get into order
A bad smell from the lavatory
Flows under the concrete floor and at the border

By the sea our chain fence
Was ripped out on a Friday night
A pine tree fell in the same storm
Destroying the garden and try as we might

The insurers won't pay, they say
'You bought that fence over ten years ago
It's your fault, suckers'
Even though they well know

The tempest was an act of God
What's more, inevitably, the Wi-Fi's screwed
Freebox can't come for a week
I wait on the phone for some dude

Meanwhile down our front steps
Someone's now driven a car
Our neighbour's daughter was drunk
Is it me? Am I getting bourgeois?

I don't remember, someone tell me,
Was life always like this?
Is our crime to have looked for sanctuary?
A house by the sea in France! Bliss!

Into the pool fall the pines from the trees
Clogging the filters but not
As bad as the flowers dead on the pool-house roof
Because of the watering system the gardener forgot

To turn on, and by the way, don't use the electric kettle
At the same time as the toaster
Because then the circuits and fuses will jump
And all at once you'll boast a

Total blackout from the box
At the far end of the drive
By the gate which doesn't have a
Padlock and for the first time I've

Realised this place is no different
Just the same as elsewhere
Chaos bubbling under and over
And, seriously, what hope is there

Of hoisting yourself somehow
To a place of composure less extreme?
Still, it's Provence–Alpes–Côte d'Azur, it's hot, it's summer
And we're living the dream

There's no peace, is there? And there's no calm
There's no place excluded from the tides of life
Here we are preparing for the next devastating misfortune
Me, my family, my friends, my wife

LONG STORY SHORT

If you ask me how I spend my life
I'd say dogging my father's footsteps
Today I'm in Cape Town
And all I can think about
Is how he came here

Singapore, Mumbai, Auckland
Where can I go that he didn't?

I'm so keen to avoid him, I suppose
Because dressed in his naval uniform
Bald, he sailed away from his wife and family
Laughed at jokes which weren't funny
Put himself first on all occasions
Rubbed his hands in near-constant embarrassment
Was never sighted without a pink gin
A Senior Service and a racist judgement

Am I him?

I was once eating Chinese
In the docks in Sydney
When outside a first-floor window
One of his ships glided by
So close I could almost touch it

When I was twelve
We went on holiday to Majorca
So we could meet his boat
And he could thereby
Make a reluctant admission in Palma
Eating paella while a guitarist played
That his children existed

In Cape Town the warehouses,
The junk shops, the containers,
The wreck of rust, the scuffed golf clubs
In old cloth bags with leather lining,
The model cars, the gadgetry,
The mountain six times older

Than the Himalayas
The air, the light, the blue sky
The scrubland, the Dutch churches
The corniches, the colonial hotels
The white fish criss-crossed with grill marks,
The fretwork and raffia chairs
All have one message

However far I travel
Dad was here first

A THEORY OF EVIL

Stupid souls believe there's no such thing as evil
The unwary imagine everyone means well
I'm all for the decline of judgemental religions
But I'm much less sure about the death of hell

We're divided. Why do we refuse to acknowledge it?
Why do we secretly suspect our enemies are right?
They aren't. And yes, I do believe we all have enemies
It isn't always darkest before the light

Of course, we all agree the heart has its reasons
And I admire those who can draw the poison of life
But poison there is.
Warn friends. People come disguised in charm
To silence others, to do them harm

DEATH ON WHEELS

Coming to roundabouts, cyclists in London
    are regularly killed
Going under the wheels of trucks
Or carried along beneath the undercarriages of buses
Like plastic bags
For a hundred and fifty yards without the bus driver
    knowing they're there

Cyclists are envoys, emissaries
Dispatched each day to reduce the city to a human scale
One by one they're destroyed

The intersection at King's Cross or the junction of Lambeth
    Bridge beside MI5
Are the pressure points
Propitiatory
Where the city bears down on its citizens
The city wipes cyclists off its windscreen like bugs
The massacre goes on
No attempt is made to alter these places
Their deaths are a way of reminding us who we are

One day soon everything will be city
Boston will be New York
São Paolo will be Rio

Birmingham will be London
One place

One day soon everything will be suburb
One part of the sprawl will simply be part of another
But inside men and women on bikes
Will set off
Without tin skins
Moving between the high sides of lorries
Waiting to be crushed

SAME AGAIN, PLEASE: 2001

I would like to think I have twenty more years
Assuming of course I don't get cancer
I drink a lot
And friends who drink have cancer of the throat
If it's not throat, it's prostate
There's also the Americans who seem intent on making us
    a target
For all sorts of people who would not otherwise hate us

Aged thirty-seven I had twenty more years, as it turns out
During which I wrote fourteen plays and met my wife
At this point I would settle again for twenty
If they could get me twenty
Twenty would do

THE AGEING PROCESS

It feels like a parody
When you reach down
To pick something off the floor
It feels like your body
It doesn't feel like you

I have started to sweat
My body sweats involuntarily
As though cleansing itself
For no reason
Because my body has developed
A mind of its own

After seventy years
The relationship between
You and your body has become uncoupled
It behaves in a different way
To you

The old man in the mirror is not you
He does not resemble you
I am responsible for this man
I have to look after him
At any time he may fall

When he goes out, he is not to be trusted
Mind you I was never to be trusted

SYNAPTIC SNAP

Synaptic snap and verbal vim
Are what the poet requires
Proleptic zeugma and syllepsis
Embellish his desires

Bathetic smooth soft landings
Haunt his every thought
But it's hard to think of enjambment
When your bank account's at nought

It's sharp and stony on Parnassus
Ingravescent is the path
But feeling fixed in language
The resplendent aftermath

FILM FUN

'Turn over.' 'Action.' 'Cut.' Everyone waits
Because I'm the director and what I say goes
Everyone's agreed to play a collusive game: Let's pretend
I'm the man who for the next eight weeks knows

'Going again.' 'Dolly slower this time.' 'Reload.'
   'Hair in the gate.'
The crew efficiently clicking their heels. In fact,
   they're passing the buck
Because they know better than me, for all the slick
   deployment of argot
Often as not, a good film is a matter of luck

I had the best teachers. Louis Malle. Daldry. Schepisi. Frears.
Now I'm blithely rattling along the identical tramline myself.
'Continuous day.' 'Golden hour.' 'It's a wrap.' 'First assembly.'
   'Second assembly.' 'Rough cut.'
'Fine cut.' 'Picture lock.' 'World premiere.' 'Release.' Shelf.

SEVENTY

Three score and ten is it, says Yahweh
Three score and ten is all you're allowed
After three score and ten you're finished
Whoever you are, humble or proud

Don't waste your breath asking for longer
Man was allotted seventy from when he began
Complain all you like, forget it, it's official
Take it from Yahweh – seventy's man's natural span

Though he listens both to saints and to sinners
On this particular point, see, Yahweh is firm
'I created the world with strict regulations
And this is one I'm enforcing long term'

Men may succumb to malfunctioning prostates
For a woman the killer inside is the breast
But for both genders obsolescence is programmed
No wonder mankind is depressed

You're not there when the planet's created
And you're not there when the planet expires
You'll live like the average mosquito
Because that's all that Yahweh requires

Yahweh picks you up and he looks at you
Having looked, he soon puts you down
Don't imagine you're of any significance
For him, you're a shrug, a fancy, a frown

His joke is to make everyone different
So each one feels they have some special aim
But it's only Yahweh making his special mischief
Because each of us ends up the same

He's no interest in your particular pleadings
For your feelings he gives not a whit
If you suggest you deserve something better
He wipes you out and that's it

You can choose to be burnt or be buried
Or pulled through the streets in elaborate display
Don't fool yourself: it's simply a means of postponing
An unending future of rot and decay

It's hard to accept of my Nicole
Whom I loved more than any woman I knew
The idea that she too is mortal
Seems too absurd to be possibly true

Look in her eyes and see her laughter
Look in her face and see her delight
Then contemplate the indefensible system
That condemns her to go out like a light

There's no way of accepting the arrangements
They seem devised for maximum pain
We give our whole lives to another
Then we never see them again

Face it: we're victims of a cruel sense of humour
The only thing God truly loves is a joke
The rest of the stuff is kerfuffle
Whether you've lived as a bird or a bloke

Come, Nicole, come close and embrace me
Let me swim in the pool of your gaze
Forget Yahweh. Fuck him! Tell him from both of us
Seventy's nothing these days

BUDLEIGH

Budleigh Salterton's full of men who love their wives
This small town was purpose-built, it seems,
    for uxorious parade
I've never seen so many dignified old gents with beards
    hold hands with grey-haired ladies
For them love's not love unless it's extravagantly displayed

How surprising coming from London in the warm September
    sunshine
To walk among so many couples who'll always love
    each other most
Life brought them close. The closeness of the end much
    closer still.
The promenade's packed. They stroll on, blissful, soon fossils
    on love's Jurassic coast

STILL AROUND

It doesn't look as if my wife will die soon
Her mother's one-oh-one and shows no signs of fading
Nicole's genetic mix is programmed for longevity
And needs no pharmaceutical persuading

Because it has its own momentum. You can't help
Noticing that virtue, in the face of determined opposition,
Finds its own way through, like water forging a riverbed
Straight, unhurried, direct, untroubled and without condition

Lawrence called it the life force, but that isn't quite it,
Is it? There's an ugliness implicit in that notion
As though the things we don't like were immoral.
I don't agree. This is more like forward motion

So respectfully I'd prefer to point out something different
People who are self-confident are almost never wise
They're usually stupid. They're missing the complexity
Of life. So I must record my backflipping surprise

Twenty-eight years ago, I met a woman without self-doubt
Who was also intelligent. Result? Today a stale idea is sprung
Don't bullshit me please as I celebrate Nicole's durability
It isn't always true, you know, that the good die young

THE DEATH OF EVERYBODY

I'm reaching the point where I'm hearing of
The death of everybody
How can I mourn an individual
When everybody's dead?

For anyone who did anything public
There's an unwelcome change in the air
My friend Philip Roth was a misogynist
And a bully, so says his biographer
Mike Nichols was addicted to crack cocaine
And money – a biographer again –
Overleaf, I read that Patricia Highsmith was
Anti-Semitic, glowering and drunk

It's new, this thing of nobody being forgiven
A game in which ladders are broken
And only snakes fed
I wasn't invited to the meeting at which it was agreed
That people should altogether stop liking each other

For most of us it's a struggle to be good
It doesn't come naturally
It's easy to be a saint if that's the temperament
You're born with
But for many of us, our given nature is something
We have to overcome

The harder the endeavour,
The more inspiring, I think

Of course, if you yourself were not born
But dropped by an angel on the great righteous heights
Perhaps you feel qualified to calibrate
The rest of us
Being faultless yourself, you have an
Oenophile's nose for the corked bottle
From the back of the cellar

How lucky you are
The moral high ground is an overcrowded place these days
Haul yourself up
And judge

WORK THAT DOESN'T EXIST

'The best paintings' said Elaine de Kooning
'Are the ones one hasn't made yet.'

Is that what it's about?
What drives you on, friend?
Something?
Or the idea of something?

What pleases you?

Myself, I'm embarrassed talking airily
Expanding
Speculating about what I might be able to do
One day
If only I had the reach
If only I had the words
If only
Just as I'm embarrassed when
The talk turns to love, to justice, or to ideals

Surely these things should be there
They should run so deep that they can't be dug out
They should be things you don't have to inflate
They don't need decorating
They're too important to be pumped up with talk

Are you driven on by a dream? I'm not
I'm driven on by what's been done
I've seen what's been done and it inspires me

Do I think we could all do better?
Maybe
But in the world as it is
It would be helpful if we just did well

THANKS

Many of the essays in the first half of the book appeared in the *Guardian* when the open-minded commissioning editors included Annalena McAfee, Claire Armitstead, Lisa Allardice and Merope Mills. Working for them, you always knew that, whatever you wrote, you would appear next to some of the most interesting writers of the day. The 'Twenty-First-Century Lexicon' was written for the slow-news website Tortoise, the Lee Miller essay for the National Portrait Gallery, and the short piece on British war films for the Imperial War Museum. The memoir of Louis Malle was written for the matchless Anna Wintour at American *Vogue*. The essay on Joan Didion was an introduction to the Vintage edition of her play *The Year of Magical Thinking*. Trinity College Oxford asked me to give their annual lecture in memory of Richard Hillary. The interrogation of populism was published in the *New Statesman*. 'Influence' was first printed in *Index on Censorship*.

Faber is a publishing house which retains its editors just as surely as it retains its authors. I have had four excellent editors in over fifty years – Frank Pike, Tracey Scoffield, Peggy Paterson and, for the last twenty years, Dinah Wood. Working under the eye of Dinah's impeccable judgement has been a special joy.